POLITICAL PARTIES

David Simpson

Hodder & Stoughton

A MEMBER OF THE HODDER HEADLINE GROUP

DEDICATION

To my wife, Audrey.

Orders: please contact Bookpoint Ltd, 39 Milton Park, Abingdon, Oxon OX14 4TD. Telephone: (44) 01235 400414, Fax: (44) 01235 400454. Lines are open from 9.00–6.00, Monday to Saturday, with a 24 hour message answering service. Email address: orders@bookpoint.co.uk

A catalogue record for this title is available from The British Library

ISBN 0 340 774 576

First published 2000
Impression number 10 9 8 7 6 5 4 3 2 1
Year   2005 2004 2003 2002 2001 2000

Cover photo from Corbis/Pawel Libera

Typeset by Transet Limited, Coventry, England.
Printed in Great Britain for Hodder & Stoughton Educational, a division of Hodder Headline plc, 338 Euston Road, London NW1 3BH by Redwood Books, Trowbridge, Wilts.

CONTENTS

ACKNOWLEDGEMENTS

Thanks to Audrey Simpson for all her work. Thanks also to Luke Hacker, Chris Loades and their colleagues for their work in the publishing of this book. The publishers would like to thank PA photos, Popperfoto, Corbis, Pawel Libera, David Brenchley and Kieran Doherty for permission to reproduce the photographs on page 62 and the cover. They would also like to thank the Party headquarters of the Liberal Democrats, Labour and Conservative parties for permission to reproduce their logos on the cover.

1

INTRODUCTION

The focus of this book is on 'major' political parties which refers in the main to the Conservative and Labour parties, but this does not exclude the Liberal Democrat party, the nationalist parties nor parties of Northern Ireland being referred to as examples.

It looks at **the role of political parties**, including the functions of political parties (Chapter 2), different party systems (Chapter 3) and the ideological traditions of the major parties (Chapter 4). Political parties are important not only because of the range of functions they carry out, but also because different party systems have implications for the political process in general.

The roles and functions of the major political parties are considered also in terms of the contemporary programmes being promoted by the parties (Chapter 5), party structure and organisation (Chapter 6), the merits of the state fully funding political parties in the light of recent scandals and declining party membership (Chapter 7). Ideology, policies, organisation and membership are related to each other. For example, an important feature of the Labour Party's modernisation strategy was the drive to increase the number of individual party members. A key strategic goal of the process was to bypass the traditional Labour Party activists by opening up decision–making to the wider party membership. Thus, organisational reforms were linked to a policy agenda. The modernisation process in the Conservative Party after 1997 followed a similar pattern. William Hague argued that an expanded membership was dependent upon members being offered a meaningful role within the party. The reorganisation of the Conservative Party had wider policy implications.

There is evidence of the declining health of parties as membership continues to decline. Individual membership of the Conservative Party and the Labour Party has declined from the early 1950s when a Conservative Party membership of 2.8 million and a Labour Party membership of 1 million was claimed. By the end of the century membership of the Conservative Party had declined to under 400,000. Individual membership of the Labour Party had declined up until 1994. The effects of an active membership recruitment strategy turned out to be very successful. By 1997 the membership had reached 405,238 (Labour Party, 1998a), a 40 per cent increase over the 1994 membership. However, it was down to 388,000 by the end of 1998 (Labour Party, 1999). There has also been a decline in the strength of Labour and Conservative partisanship (see Robinson, *Voting Behaviour and Electoral Systems*, 1998, Hodder and Stoughton, part of the Access to Politics series, pp. 37–41). In addition to people being less willing either to join or identify with parties, there are other explanations of party decay which are related to the nature of contemporary society and political behaviour. As society has become more specialised and diversified, the number of pressure groups has grown. New pressure groups, particularly cause groups such as environmental ones, have been increasingly important in setting the political agenda (see Simpson, 1999, *Pressure Groups*, part of the Access to Politics series, pp. 6–9). A new form of the politics of anti-partyism has emerged which Liplow and Seyd describe as 'techno-populism'. Factors reflecting this situation include the use of private polls and focus groups in place of the views of the parties' mass membership.

However, the importance of parties to the political system should be stressed. They 'fulfil important collective functions in an increasingly atomised, individualised society. The danger today is of the atomised individual at the mercy of powerful elites' (Seyd, 1998). For the overwhelming majority power comes from organisation. Without organisation and structure the new means of communication are 'at worst the vehicles of demagogues and small, well–organised groups which rely only on themselves … individuals are only weak atoms. Disaggregating parties… empowers elites' (Lipow and Seyd, 1996).

Nevertheless, the future role of parties must reflect the patterns of living in modern society and be based on the new means of communication. Parties in the 21st century should relate to the new pressure groups, and teach their members how to use the new means of communication. A bottom-up party, based upon local branches, linked with pressure groups, has the possibility of transforming a top-down society into a bottom-up one. Links must be two-way, rather than dominated by the party, even though the party must remain the place in which disparate interests and causes can come together.

2

THE FUNCTIONS OF POLITICAL PARTIES

Introduction

THIS CHAPTER WILL look at the functions of political parties, distinguishing between political parties and pressure groups and assessing the role of minor parties in the UK political system. It will discuss the relationship between political parties and democracy.

Key points
- The function of political parties.
- The distinction between political parties and pressure groups.
- The role of minor parties.
- The relationship between political parties and democracy.

THE FUNCTIONS OF POLITICAL PARTIES

The main functions of political parties are identified by Heywood (1997) as:

Representation
Political parties respond to and articulate the view of both members and the voters.

Elite formation and recruitment
Parties provide political leaders from within their ranks. Contestants in a presidential election are usually party leaders, while in parliamentary systems of government the leader of the largest part in Parliament normally becomes prime minister. Other ministerial posts are usually filled by senior party figures, though

exceptions are found in presidential systems like that of the USA which allow non-party ministers to be appointed.

Goal formulation

Political parties have traditionally been one of the means through which societies set collective goals. Parties play this role because, in the process of seeking power, they formulate programmes of government with a view to attracting popular support.

Interest articulation and aggregation

In the process of developing collective goals parties also help to articulate and aggregate the various interests found in society. Indeed, parties often develop as vehicles through which pressure groups advance or defend their various interests. For example, the Labour Party was created by the trade–union movement with the aim of achieving working-class political representation. Parties in the USA in the late nineteenth and early twentieth centuries recruited immigrant groups in order to broaden their electoral base.

Socialisation and mobilisation

Through internal debate and discussion, as well as campaigning and electoral competition, parties are important agents of socialisation. Major parties in the UK play no less significant a role in encouraging groups to play by the rules of the game, thus mobilising support for the political system itself. For example, the emergence of the Labour Party in the twentieth century was an important means of integrating the working class into industrial society.

Organisation of government

Parties help with the formation of governments to the extent that, in parliamentary systems of government like the UK, it is possible to talk of 'party government'.

Parties are particularly important in the UK political system in which parliamentary discipline provides the essential underpinning of the executive (see Simpson, 1998). Seyd and Whitely (1995) speculate about the effects of a weak party system developing, as for example in the USA, on executive politics in Britain:

- Majority support coalitions would have to be constructed around every political issue. Unlike the presidential executive, Cabinet government has no independent electoral base.
- Special interests would increasingly begin to dominate government policy-making. When the party system is weak, special interests become strong. Thus in the absence of institutions whose main function is to aggregate interests over a broad spectrum, narrow interests take over.
- The hand of 'political entrepreneurs' who may have the resources to, in effect, buy themselves representation in government, would be strengthened. An

example of this was Ross Perot in the USA. Such figures build their support on the basis of populist appeals but lack the experience, or the organisational base on which to govern if they do succeed in winning office. Thus their track record in government is usually poor and tends to weaken the legitimacy of the policy–making process.

POLITICAL PARTIES AND PRESSURE GROUPS

(see Simpson, *Pressure Groups*, 1999).

- Political parties 'aim to exercise government power by winning political office' (Heywood, 1997), whereas pressure groups 'seek to exert influence from outside, rather than to win or exercise government power' (Heywood, 1997).

  However, minor parties may 'use elections more to gain a platform than to win power' (Heywood, 1997). The aim of exercising government power by winning political office is not always realistic. For example, the Natural Law Party (which put up 195 candidates in the 1997 general election) believes in yogic flying and the solution of national and international ills by the development of cosmic consequences.

- Parties 'typically adopt a broad focus, addressing each of the major areas of government policy' (Heywood, 1997), whereas pressure groups 'typically have a narrow issue focus, in that they are usually concerned with a specific cause or the interests of a particular group' (Heywood, 1997).

  However, minor parties 'may have a single–issue focus' (Heywood, 1997), thus resembling pressure groups. For example, the United Kingdom Independence Party (UKIP) is dedicated to the withdrawal of the UK from the European Union.

THE ROLE OF MINOR PARTIES

Minor parties play a role in the evolution of the major parties' ideas. For example, both major parties began to examine seriously the prospect of devolution following the rise of the nationalist parties in Scotland and Wales in the late 1960s. Plaid Cymru won the Carmarthen by–election in 1966 and the Scottish National Party won the Hamilton by–election in 1967. The Labour Party's interest became even more urgent as the threat to its electoral heartlands in Scotland became more obvious. The SNP achieved 30 per cent of the Scottish vote and 11 seats in the October 1974 general election. Such influence does not even require the capture of parliamentary seats, merely enough votes to jeopardise seats held by the party in government. For example, the Green Party's 15 per cent vote in the 1989 European elections forced environmental issues to the forefront of the major parties' agenda, even though the 'Greens' achieved no representation at all at national or European level.

Changes in voting behaviour after 1970 enhanced the potential of minor parties as a force both upon and within UK governments. Class dealignment and partisan dealignment resulted in the decline of the two–party system (see Simpson, 1998). The increased likelihood of no party having an absolute majority in the House of Commons offered minor parties the prospect of the sort of pivotal influence enjoyed by minor parties in other European countries. For example, the Free Democrat Party (FDP) in Germany has exerted a moderating influence in coalition with alternately the Christian Democratic Union (CDU) and the Social Democratic Party (SPD). In the UK, the Lib–Lab pact of 1977–8 gave the Liberal Party some influence in government decision-making in return for keeping Callaghan's Labour government in office. The 'negative' effectiveness of the pact was shown, for example, in curbing ambitions for further nationalisation and for achieving expenditure restraint. Councils in which no single party has overall control have remained a significant feature of UK local politics, in spite of an electoral system favouring single–party government.

Even though the Labour Party won a landslide Parliamentary majority in 1997, the Liberal Democrats were included on a Cabinet committee dealing with constitutional reform. The first elections in Great Britain held under systems of proportional representation took place in May 1999 for both the Scottish Parliament and the Welsh Assembly. No party had an absolute majority of seats, the Labour Party being forced into a coalition with the Liberal Democrats in Scotland and forming a minority administration in Wales. At European level, the Green Party and the UKIP secured their first representation in the European Parliament as a result of the election held under proportional representation in June 1999.

THE RELATIONSHIP BETWEEN POLITICAL PARTIES AND DEMOCRACY

(on the nature of democracy, see Simpson, 1998, Chapter 4).

Representation
Political parties help to ensure that government heeds the needs and wishes of the larger society.

However:

- Parties seek to shape public opinion as well as respond to it.
- The range of electoral choice is often narrow. A systematic analysis of the 1970 and 1974 manifestos shows that more than half of all manifesto pledges are non-partisan (see table 1). Many of the differences between manifestos stem from what Rose calls 'talking past' each other , as in the 1951 election manifestos. Rose claims that manifesto differences are deliberately exaggerated by their proponents, with policy differences being mainly derived from detail and emphasis rather than ideological principles.

Table 1: *Partisan and Nonpartisan Manifesto Pledges, 1970–74*				
	NONPARTISAN		PARTISAN	
	N	%	N	%
1970				
Conservatives	42	45	52	55
Labour	56	67	27	33
Totals	98	55	79	45
1974				
Conservatives	83	66	43	34
Labour	51	48	55	52
Totals	134	58	98	42

SOURCE: *Rose, 1984, p.69*

For Rose, this tendency to agree behind the adversarial rhetoric was a product of how party policy really worked in a modern democracy. Parties are primarily interested in attaining office, which means reflecting the views of substantial portions of voters, especially those 'floating' voters not aligned to any one party. These non-aligned voters almost by definition tend to be 'middle of the road', which tends to lessen the differences between the major parties. If there are fundamental differences between them, for example, as they were in 1983, this normally means that one party (the Labour Party in this case) has failed to reflect properly the concerns of the middle-ground voter, thus leading to a catastrophic defeat. Rose believed it to be no coincidence that during the 1945–70 period, in which each major party governed for roughly seventeen years, the policy differences between them were marginal. Conversely, during the 1979–97 period, in which one party, the Conservative Party, was dominant, the differences seemed to be substantial. If there is to be more than one party of government, then the policy differences between the major parties cannot be extensive. If a party is elected on a radical manifesto, for example as in 1945 and 1979, it is probably because it has sensed a similar shift in public opinion. Parties thus respond to rather than instigate change.

- The image of voters as well informed, rational and issue-orientated is questionable (see Robinson, 1998).

Elite formation and recruitment

Parties provide a training ground for politicians, equipping them with skills, knowledge and experience. However, the stranglehold that parties exert over government offices can be criticised for ensuring that political leaders are drawn from a relatively small pool of talent – the senior figures in a handful of major parties. In the USA this stranglehold has been weakened by the widespread use of primary elections, which reduce the control that a party has over the process of candidate selection and nomination.

Goal formulation

Political parties formulate coherent sets of policy options that give the electorate a choice amongst realistic and achievable goals. This function is most clearly carried out by parties in parliamentary systems of government which are able to claim a mandate to implement their policies if elected. It can also occur in presidential systems with usually non-programmatic parties, for example the Republican Party's 'Contract with America' in the US congressional elections of 1994.

However:

- The tendency towards what Kirchheimer (1996) termed 'catch–all parties', that is parties that drastically reduce their ideological goals in order to appeal to the largest number of voters, and the fact that election campaigns increasingly stress personality and image over policy and issues, has generally reduced the impact that parties have on policy formulation.
- Party programmes are almost certain to be modified by pressure from the civil service and pressure groups, as well as in the light of domestic and international circumstances, policy implementation being usually carried out by bureaucracies rather than parties.
- Most manifesto pledges have in fact been acted upon. For example, the 1970–74 Conservative government 'fulfilled at least 80 per cent of its manifesto pledges, and showed some evidence of action in another 10 per cent of cases' (Rose, 1984). Faced with a very difficult parliamentary situation in which it often could not be sure of a majority, the 1974–79 Labour government nevertheless 'acted unambiguously upon 54 per cent of all its manifesto commitments and gave evidence of action upon another 19 per cent' (see Table 2).

  However, 'the great bulk of government legislation is prepared independently of manifesto commitments. More than three-quarters of all the legislation that a government introduces is derived from the ongoing policy process in Whitehall' (Rose, 1984). Civil servants consult with pressure groups to see what can be done about problems of concern to government departments. Unexpected events, such as sterling and foreign crises, sometimes force a governing party to react without the guidance of a manifesto commitment or the advice of a departmental committee.

  Kelly's authors generally agree that 'many landmarks in post–war British history would have occurred whichever party was in power and would have elicited a broadly similar response', the sterling crises of 1947 and 1949, the Suez crisis of 1956, the oil crisis of 1973, the International Monetary Fund's intervention in 1976, and the devaluations of 1967 and 1992 being conspicuous examples (Kelly, 1999a).

  Rose argued that the direction of the British economy was primarily influenced by what he called 'long–term' secular trends independent of party' and not by the movement of parties in and out of office. There were no significant differences in economic policy inputs.

Table 2: *How Parties Act upon Their Manifestos, 1970–79*							
	Conservative Government 1970–74				Labour Government 1974–79		
	Acted Upon	Ambig-uous	No Action	Oppo-site	Acted Upon	Ambig-uous	No Action	Oppo-site
The Economy	22	2	5	1	26	4	9	0
Environment	13	1	1	0	8	4	5	1
Home Office and Parliamentary	11	3	1	0	5	2	5	0
Health and Social Security	17	2	1	0	10	4	1	0
Education and Science	7	0	0	0	2	3	5	0
Foreign Affairs and Defence	5	1	0	0	3	3	2	0
Agriculture	2	1	0	0	3	0	0	0
Totals	77 (80%)	10 (10%)	8 (8%)	1 (1%)	57 (54%)	20 (19%)	27 (26%)	1 (1%)

Source: *Rose, 1984, p.65*

Interest articulation and aggregation

The fact that political parties invariably articulate the demands of a multitude of groups forces them to aggregate these interests, by drawing them together into a coherent whole, balancing competing interests against each other. However, not all interests are articulated, those of small groups, the relatively poor and the politically disorganised being the most vulnerable to exclusion.

Socialisation and mobilisation

The issues parties choose to focus on helps to set the political agenda, the values and attitudes that they articulate becoming part of the larger political culture. However, the capacity of parties to socialise and mobilise has been brought into doubt by evidence of partisan dealignment and growing disenchantment with conventional parties. The problem that parties have is that, to some extent, they themselves are socialised by the experience of government, making them, it appears, less effective in engaging partisan sympathies and attracting emotional attachments.

Organisation of government

Parties give governments a degree of stability and coherence, especially if the members of the government are drawn from a single party and are therefore united by common sympathies and attachments. They facilitate cooperation between the two main branches of government, the legislature and the executive. This is effectively guaranteed in parliamentary systems of government by the fact that the government is formed from the party or parties having majority control of Parliament. Even in presidential systems of government the president can wield some influence, if not control, through an appeal to party unity. Parties provide a vital source of opposition and criticism both inside and outside of government. This helps to ensure that government policy is more thoroughly scrutinised and therefore more likely to be workable.

SUMMARY

The functions of political parties include their role as a mechanism of representation, the formation of political elites and recruitment into politics, the formulation of goals, the articulation and aggregation of interests, the socialisation and mobilisation of the electorate, and the organisation of government.

Political parties aim to exercise government power by winning political office, whereas pressure groups seek to exert influence from outside, rather than to win or exercise government power. However, minor parties may use elections more to gain a platform than to win power. Parties typically adopt a broad focus, addressing each of the major areas of government policy, whereas pressure groups typically have a narrow issue focus, in that they are usually concerned with a specific cause or the interests of a particular group. However, minor parties may have a single-issue focus, thus resembling pressure groups.

Political parties promote democracy by:

- ensuring that government heeds the needs and wishes of the larger society;
- providing a training ground for politicians;
- giving the electorate a choice amongst realistic and achievable goals;
- balancing competing interests against each other;
- helping to set the political agenda, the values and attitudes that they articulate becoming part of the larger political culture;
- giving governments a degree of stability and coherence, facilitating cooperation between the two branches of government and providing a vital source of opposition and criticism, both inside and outside government.

However, they seek to shape public opinion as well as respond to it, the range of electoral choice is often narrow, the image of voters as well informed, rational and issue-orientated questionable; political leaders are drawn from a relatively small pool of talent; the tendency towards de-ideologised catch-all parties, and the fact that election campaigns increasingly stress personality and image over policy and issues, has generally reduced the impact that parties have on policy formulation, party programmes moreover almost certain to be modified by pressure from the civil service and pressure groups, as well as in the light of domestic and international circumstances, policy implementation being usually carried out by bureaucracies rather than parties; not all interests are articulated; the capacity of parties to socialise and mobilise has been brought into doubt by evidence of partisan dealignment and growing disenchantment with conventional politics.

Revision hints

Make sure you have a knowledge of the functions of political parties, understanding the distinction between political parties and pressure groups, and the role of minor parties in the UK political system. You should be able to discuss the relationship between political parties and democracy.

Exam hints

Answering structured questions on The Functions of Political Parties

1 (a) Outline the key functions of political parties.   (5 marks)
   (b) In what ways do political parties promote democracy?   (10 marks)

   (c) What are the main points of disagreement between the major UK political parties?   (15 marks)

   (d) How internally united is each major party?   (20 marks)

                                                                      Total: 50 marks

(Specimen Papers with Mark Schemes, Edexcel GCE Government and Politics, Unit Test 1 – People and Politics, Advanced Subsidiary/Advanced, 2000 Edexcel.)

Questions (a) and (b) can be answered from material contained in this Chapter.

In answer to (a) show understanding of key functions of political parties including representation, elite formation and recruitment, goal formulation, interest articulation and aggregation, socialisation and mobilisation, organisation of government.

In answer to (b) analyse a variety of ways in which political parties are seen to promote democracy including their ability to promote participation through membership and office holding, their capacity to inform the electorate through policy debate and argument, and their ability, via competitive elections, to translate public opinion into go vernment policy.

Practice questions

1 (a) How do political parties differ from pressure groups?
   (b) Why is it sometimes difficult to distinguish between political parties and
        pressure groups.
2 Assess the role of minor parties in the UK political system.

3

PARTY SYSTEMS

Introduction

THIS CHAPTER WILL look at different party systems. It will explain their implications for the political process in general. Finally, it will assess the changing UK party system.

Key points

- Party systems.
- The implications of different party systems for the political process in general.
- The changing UK party system.

THE DEFINITION OF A PARTY SYSTEM

A **party system** is defined by Sartori (1976) as precisely '*the system of interactions resulting from inter-party competition*'.

A one–party system

Heywood (1997) defines a **one–party system** as one in which 'a single party enjoys a monopoly of power through the exclusion of all other parties (by political or constitutional means)'. He identifies two rather different types of one–party system. The first type has been found in communist states where a single, 'ruling' party, the communist party, has directed and controlled virtually all the institutions and aspects of society. Examples are the now-collapsed communist states, like the Soviet Union, and surviving ones such as China, Cuba and North Korea. The second type of one–party system is associated with anti-colonial nationalism and state consolidation in the developing world, usually built around the dominant role of a charismatic leader and drawing whatever ideological identification it has possessed from the views of the leader. Examples are Kwame Nkrumah in Ghana, Julius Nyerere in Tanzania and Robert Mugabe in Zimbabwe.

A dominant–party system

A **dominant–party system** should be distinguished from a one–party system. It is open and pluralistic, at least in the sense that a number of parties compete for power in regular and popular elections. In other words, the general public possesses the constitutional ability to remove the government from office, but chooses not to use it. A dominant–party system is, therefore, 'a competitive party system dominated by a single major party that consequently enjoys a prolonged period of government power' (Heywood, 1994).

O'Leary (1994) defines a dominant–party system according to four criteria:

- A party must regularly win more seats in elections to the legislature than its opponents.
- It must be able to stay in government on a regular basis.
- It must govern continuously for a long time.
- It must be ideologically dominant: it must be capable of using government to shape public policy so that the nature of the state and society over which it presides is fundamentally changed.

This definition runs into problems, however, notably in deciding how long a party must govern continuously for it to be considered 'dominant'. Three or four consecutive general–election victories? A decade or a decade and a half?

A classic example of a dominant–party system was Japan between 1955 and 1993:

- The Liberal Democratic Party (LDP) regularly won more seats in elections to the House of Representatives, the lower chamber of the Japanese legislature, than its opponents.
- It was able to stay in government on a regular basis, having failed to gain an overall majority in the House of Representatives in 1976, 1979 and 1983 only.
- It governed continuously for 38 years.
- It was ideologically dominant, reflecting the powerful appeal of the party's neo-Confucian principles of duty and obligation in the still–traditional Japanese countryside, as well as the strong links it had forged with business élites.

A two–party system

Heywood (1997) identifies a **two–party system** by three criteria:

- Although a number of minor parties exist, only two parties enjoy sufficient electoral and legislative strength to have a realistic prospect of winning government power.
- The large party is able to rule alone (usually on the basis of a legislative majority).

- Power alternates between these parties; both are 'electable', the opposition serving as an alternative government.

An example of a two–party system is the USA:

- Only the Democratic Party and the Republican Party enjoy sufficient electoral strength to have a realistic prospect of winning government power.
- The larger party is able to rule alone (though the presidential system allows one party to rule alone at the White House while the other has a legislative majority in Congress).
- Power alternates between the two parties.

A multi–party system

Heywood defines a **multi–party system** as one characterised by 'competition amongst more than two parties reducing the chances of single–party government' (1997). For example, in Germany competition amongst the Christian Democratic Union (CDU), the Social Democratic Party (SPD) and the Free Democratic Party (FDP) reduces the chances of single–party government.

THE IMPLICATIONS OF PARTY SYSTEMS FOR THE POLITICAL PROCESS IN GENERAL

Party systems shape the broader political process in various ways:

- *Choice*: They influence the range and nature of choice to the electorate.
- *Stability*: They affect the stability of governments.
- *Accountability*: They structure the relationship between the executive and the legislature.
- *Conflict or consensus*: They establish a bias in favour of either conflict or consensus, and shape the general character of the political culture.

A one–party system

The justification for both the communist party's monopoly of power and its supervision of state and social institutions lies in vanguardism, the belief of Lenin in the need for a party to lead and guide the proletariat (the working masses) towards the fulfilment of their revolutionary destiny. The 'ruling' party that developed out of an independence movement in the developing world proclaimed the overriding need for nation building and economic development.

However, vanguardism has been criticised for being deeply elitist and providing the seed from which Stalinism, Stalin's brutal political discipline, grew. Parties in the developing world are weakly organised, and they play at best only a peripheral role in the process of policy making, but their monopolistic position helps to entrench authoritarianism and to keep alive the danger of corruption.

A dominant–party system

Apart from the tendency towards stability, a **dominant–party system** is usually seen as disadvantageous. It 'poses a threat to the political process and is corrosive of the democratic spirit' (Heywood, 1993)

- *The distinction between party and state breaks down.* When power ceases to alternate 'an insidious process of politicisation takes place and the distinction between party and state becomes blurred' (Heywood, 1993). In Japan, for example, the LDP's status as a 'permanent' government led to an unhealthily close relationship with the state bureaucracy. About one–quarter of the party's members of the upper House, the Diet, were former civil servants, creating a 'revolving door' that made political neutrality in the bureaucracy virtually impossible.

- *Dominant–party complacency, arrogance and even corruption.* When a party starts to regard itself as a 'permanent' government, the result can be either complacency or arrogance. In extreme cases, complacency can lead to corruption. For example, the course of Japanese politics was regularly interrupted by scandals, usually involving allegations of corruption. The decline of the LDP in the 1990s was closely linked to such allegations, the most serious threats to LDP dominance resulting from events such as the Lockhead bribery scandal in 1979 which provoked the resignation and later imprisonment of Prime Minister Tanaka.

- *Weak and ineffective opposition.* When parties are no longer regarded as genuine rivals for government power, their views and opinions, however well expressed, no longer carry weight and can more easily be ignored. Moreover, a prolonged period in opposition brings its own problems, including a tendency towards internal disputes and divisions, resulting from mounting frustration and the fact that the prospect of power is perhaps the best guarantee of party unity. For example, opposition to the LDP in Japan was weak and fragmented. The principal opposition party was the Japan Socialist Party, which split in 1960 with the formation of a breakaway, more right wing Democratic Socialist Party, and again in 1997 with the formation of the smaller Social Democratic Federation. There were also the Japanese Communist Party and Komeito, the political wing of an 8–million strong Buddhist sect.

- *A deferential political culture.* A dominant–party system tends to have a profound but insidious influence upon the political culture. Long periods of one–party rule engender the belief that the party is the 'natural' party of government; in the popular mind the dominant party is linked with security and stability, with the 'natural' order of things. In effect, longevity appears to invest the dominant party with a 'right' to govern, a fact that encourages 'deference, conformity and a fear of change' (Heywood, 1993).

A two–party system

A two-party system implies a system of **party government**. The key features of party government are:

- The two major parties offer the electorate a meaningful choice between rival programmes and alternative governments.
- The winning party is able to carry out its manifesto pledges without having to negotiate or compromise with coalition partners.
- Responsibility is maintained by the government's accountability to the electorate through its mandate, and because it is constantly confronted by an opposition that acts as an alternative government.

The two–party system also "creates a bias in favour of moderation, as the two contenders for power have to battle for 'floating' votes in the centre ground" (Heywood, 1997)

However, a two–party system imposes restrictions in terms of electoral and ideological choice. A choice between two programmes of policies may have been sufficient in an era of class and partisan alignments, but it has become inadequate in a period of class and partisan dealignments (see Robinson, 1998). The two–party system has displayed a periodic tendency towards adversary politics, the argument that the swing of the electoral pendulum leads to damaging policy reversals, giving rise to instability. On the other hand, two evenly matched parties are encouraged to compete for votes by outdoing each other's electoral promises, implying irresponsible government in that parties come to office on the basis of manifestos that they do not have the capacity to fulfil. Moreover, the two–party system implies 'an emphasis on conflict and argument rather than consensus and compromise' (Heywood, 1997).

A multi–party system

A multi–party system implies **coalition government**. The process of coalition formation and the dynamics of coalition maintenance ensure a broad response that cannot but take account of competing views and contending interests. For example, in Germany the liberal FDP exerts a moderating influence upon both the conservative CDU and the social democratic SPD. The multi–party system exhibits 'a bias in favour of debate, conciliation and compromise' (Heywood, 1997).

However, the tendency towards moderation and compromise may mean that a multi–party system is dominated by the political centre and is unable to offer clear ideological alternatives. It leads to the over-representation of minor parties. For example, in Germany the FDP has been permanently in government. Coalition government may be unstable. For example, in Italy postwar governments have lasted on average less than a year, though in Germany, for example, coalition government has been stable during the same period.

THE CHANGING UK PARTY SYSTEM

1945–74: two–party

- Only the Conservative Party and the Labour Party enjoyed sufficient strength amongst the electorate (see Table 4) and in the House of Commons (see Table 3) to have a realistic prospect of winning government power.
- The larger party was able to rule alone (on the basis of a legislative majority, though of only 5 in 1950 and only 4 in 1964).
- Power alternated between these parties, four times, from Conservative to Labour in 1945, Labour to Conservative in 1951, Conservative to Labour in 1964, and Labour to Conservative in 1970, though it did not alternate when the Conservative Party governed continuously for thirteen years between 1951 and 1964; it was questioned whether the Labour Party was 'electable' after its third successive election defeat in 1959 — *Must Labour Lose?* was the title of a book published in 1960 (Abrams and Rose).

Table 3: *Number of seats 1945–97*				
YEAR	CONSERVATIVE[1]	LABOUR	THIRD PARTY[2]	OTHERS[3]
1945	213	393	12	22
1950	299	315	9	2
1951	321	295	6	3
1955	345	277	6	2
1959	365	258	6	1
1964	304	317	9	–
1966	253	363	12	2
1970	330	288	6	6
Feb. 1974	297	301	14	23
Oct. 1974	277	319	13	26
1979	339	269	11	16
1983	397	209	23	21
1987	376	229	22	23
1992	336	271	20	24
1997	165	419	46	29

1 Including Ulster Unionists 1945–70.
2 The Liberal Party 1945–79, the Liberal–SDP Alliance 1983–87, the Liberal Democrats 1992–97.
3 Including Ulster Unionists Feb. 1974–97.

Table 4: *Percentage of votes cast 1945–97*				
YEAR	CONSERVATIVE[1]	LABOUR	THIRD PARTY[2]	OTHERS[3]
1945	39.8	48.3	9.1	2.8
1950	43.5	46.1	9.1	1.3
1951	48.0	48.8	2.5	0.7
1955	49.7	46.4	2.7	1.2
1959	49.4	43.8	5.9	0.9
1964	43.4	44.1	11.2	1.3
1966	41.9	47.9	8.5	1.7
1970	46.4	43.0	7.5	3.1
Feb. 1974	37.8	37.1	19.3	5.8
Oct. 1974	35.8	39.2	18.3	6.7
1979	43.9	37.0	13.8	5.3
1983	42.4	27.6	25.4	4.6
1987	42.3	30.8	22.6	4.3
1992	41.9	34.4	17.8	5.9
1997	30.7	43.2	16.8	9.3

1 Including Ulster Unionists 1945–70.
2 The Liberal Party 1945–79, the Liberal-SDP Alliance 1983–87, the Liberal Democrats 1992–97.
3 Including Ulster Unionists Feb. 1974–97.

1974–79: Multi–party

The party system was characterised by competition amongst more than two parties.

- The Liberal Party's share of the votes cast was nearly a fifth in the 1974 elections, higher than any previous postwar election (see again Table 4).
- In Scotland the SNP increased its share of the votes cast from 11.5 per cent to 21.9 per cent, and its number of seats from 1 to 7 in the February 1974 General Election. It further increased its share of the votes cast to 30.4 per cent and its number of seats to 11 at the October 1974 General Election, its best ever electoral performance at Westminster. The SNP came second in the share of the votes cast, higher than that of the Conservative Party, and it was menacingly second in 35 out of 41 Labour Party seats.
- In Wales Plaid Cymru lost a small percentage of the votes cast in both elections compared to 1970, but won two seats, its first seats at a general election, in February 1974, and gained another seat in October 1974.
- In Northern Ireland the Ulster Unionist Party has for most of its history maintained a direct organisational link with the British Conservative (and Unionist) Party, with representatives of the party in the House of Commons taking the Conservative Party whip. However, after the Conservative government of Ted Heath prorogued the Unionist-controlled devolved legislature at Stormont in 1972, the Ulster Unionists began to organise themselves as a distinct party in the House of Commons.

There was a decline in the combined Labour–Conservative electoral strength from an average of 91 per cent of the votes cast between 1945 and 1970 (ranging from 96.8 per cent in 1951 to 87.5 per cent in 1964) to 75 per cent in 1974 (see again Table 4). However, only these parties enjoyed sufficient legislative strength to have a realistic prospect of winning government power (see again Table 3).

The chances of a single–party government were reduced:

The larger party in the House of Commons, the Labour Party, was able to rule alone (though not on the basis of a legislative majority between the two general elections in 1974, and from 23 March 1976 to the general election of 1979), but the chances of single–party government were reduced. By 1977 the Labour Party was able to rule alone only on the basis of the Lib–Lab pact of 1977–8. Jim Callaghan, the Prime Minister, and David Steel, the Leader of the Liberal Party, agreed to set up a joint consultative committee under the chairmanship of the Leader of the House of Commons. This committee examined government policy and other issues prior to their coming before the House, and Liberal Party policy proposals. Regular meetings between the Chancellor of the Exchequer and the Liberal Party economic spokesman took place.

1979–97: Dominant party
- The Conservative Party regularly won more seats in elections to the House of Commons than its opponents (see again Table 3).
- It was able to stay in government on a regular basis, with four successive election victories in 1979, 1983, 1987 and 1992.
- It governed continuously for 18 years.
- It was ideologically dominant, defining free market ideology as the orthodoxy in public policy.

However, competition amongst more than two parties continued:
- Although the Liberal Party share of the votes cast fell to 13.8 per cent in 1979, that was still higher than in any postwar general election pre–1974 (see again Table 4). The Alliance of the Social Democratic Party and the Liberal Party reached over a quarter of the votes cast at the 1983 General Election, the highest third–party share of the vote since 1923, and only 2.2 per cent less than the Labour Party (see again Table 4). The Alliance share of the votes cast fell to 22.6 per cent at the 1987 General Election, but that was still higher than in any other postwar general election except 1983.
- The break up of the Alliance after the General Election of 1987 was matched by the rise of the Green Party, with 15 per cent of the votes cast for this party at the 1989 European elections.
- In Scotland the SNP averaged 16.2 per cent of the votes cast, ranging from 11.8 per cent in 1983 to 21.5 per cent in 1992. This was lower than in 1974, but significantly above pre-1974 levels. Its share of the vote in Scotland was 33 per cent in the 1994 European elections, much more than the 14.5 per cent of the

Conservative Party. In elections to the new unitary authorities in 1995, its share of the Scottish vote was 29 per cent, again much more than the 11.3 per cent of the Conservative Party.

- In Wales Plaid Cymru averaged 8.1 per cent of the votes cast. This was lower than 1970 and 1974, but significantly above the levels pre-1970. It won four seats, the highest total ever at Westminster, in 1992. Plaid Cymru became the second party both in the 1993 county council elections, winning 41 seats compared to the Conservative Party's 32 seats, and in the 1994 European elections.

- In local government, the third party (included the Liberal Party, 1979–81, the Alliance, 1981–87, the Liberal Democrats, 1988–97) made large gains. A fivefold increase in their number of councillors, from just over 1,000 in 1979 to over 5,000 in 1996, reduced the chances of one party being able to rule alone. After the 1985 local elections in England and Wales, 25 out of 45 county councils were left with no single party having overall control. This number fell to 12 out of 45 after the next county council elections in 1989, but after the 1991 local elections 108 out of 333 non-metropolitan district councils were left with 'no overall control'. Twenty-eight county councils were left with no overall control after the local elections in 1993, higher than the number in 1985. By 1993 there were more than a quarter of local authorities in England, Wales and Scotland with no overall control, 153 out of 513. The vast majority of these were in the non–metropolitan areas (Gyford, 1994).

- The decline in combined Labour–Conservative electoral strength continued. Between 1979 and 1992 the average share of the votes cast for the two main parties was still only 75 per cent, ranging from a postwar low of 70 per cent in 1983 to a post-1970 high of 80.9 per cent in 1979 (see again Table 4).

- The Conservative Party's legislative strength was based on an electoral strength of never more than 43 per cent of the votes cast between 1979 and 1992 (see Table 4). This was not only lower than the winning party in every election between 1945 and 1966, but also lower even than the 'losing' party in 1951 and 1955. Only in 1979 was it higher, marginally, than the losing party in 1959, 1964 and 1970.

- The Conservative Party won only 21 more seats in the election to the House of Commons in 1992 than its opponents. It was able to stay in government, but not on the basis of a legislative majority by the end of 1996, due to by–election losses and defections. From then on the government depended primarily on the Ulster Unionist MPs for survival (Grant, 1997).

Post–1997

At the General Election of 1997 power alternated between the two major parties, from the Conservative Party to the Labour Party. However, it was questioned whether the Conservative Party was electable — *Is Conservatism Dead?* was the title of the book published in 1997 (Gray and Willets).

The result of the 1997 General Election was a disaster for the Conservative Party. Its number of seats, 165, was its lowest since the Liberal Party landslide majority of 1906, only just managing to beat that previous record low of 157 seats. The Conservative Party's share of the votes cast was lower than in any general election since 1832.

The electoral system was now significantly biased against the Conservative Party. If the change in each party's share of the vote in each constituency had been the same as it was across the country as a whole, then the Labour Party's majority would have been 131 rather than 179 and the Liberal Democrats would have won 28 seats rather than 46. The Conservative Party won 43 seats fewer than they might otherwise have expected.

Two factors explain why the electoral system has become so biased against the Conservative Party. Fewer votes were cast in constituencies where the Labour Party was strong than where the Conservative Party was strong. More important was the fact that the votes for the Labour Party and Liberal Democrats had become more effectively distributed, while those for the Conservative Party had become less so.

Primarily due to tactical voting, both the Labour Party and the Liberal Democrats did better in seats where they were challenging the Conservative Party and thus had something to gain, while the Conservative Party lost support more heavily where it had seats to lose.

Table 5 illustrates the degree of bias in the electoral system. Assuming a uniform swing from the 1997 result, the Conservative Party would have to be more than 1 per cent ahead of the Labour Party in votes simply to deny their opponents an overall majority. In order to match the Labour Party in number of seats, the Conservative Party would need to be well over 6 per cent ahead in votes. It would need to be nearly 10 points ahead of the Labour Party to secure an overall majority.

It could not, of course, be assumed that the electoral system would remain so biased in the future. Table 5 almost undoubtedly overestimates the extent to which the Conservative Party would be disadvantaged. Some of the tactical switching between the Labour Party and the Liberal Democrats might not repeat itself at the next general election, voters no longer having the motivation to vote against an unpopular Conservative government. However, the high level of tactical voting might almost have been encouraged by the closer proximity between the Labour Party and the Liberal Democrats, and that motivation could continue.

The Labour Party succeeded in winning a landslide Parliamentary majority of 179, the biggest in postwar British politics, bigger even than the landslide of 1945 (see again Table 3). It won more seats than it had ever done before. The 10.3 per cent swing from Conservative to Labour was the largest two–party shift since

Table 5: *Targets for the Conservatives*			
	SWING	IMPLIED VOTE	
TARGET	REQUIRED %	CON %	LAB %
Deny Lab a majority	7.2	38.6	37.2
Achieve equality of seats	9.8	41.2	34.6
Win a majority	11.4	42.8	33.0
SOURCE: *NOP/BBC exit poll, 1 May 1997*			

1945, almost double the previous postwar record of 5.3 per cent, in 1979. However, the Labour Party's share of the votes cast was lower than in all elections from 1945 to 1966 (see again Table 4). This was not only lower than when it won with big majorities in 1945 and 1966 but also lower than when it won only narrowly in 1950 and 1964, and lower even than when it lost in 1951, 1955 and 1959. It was only marginally higher than when it lost in 1970. At 71.2 per cent the turnout (the percentage of the electorate who voted) was the lowest in postwar elections. It was much lower in strong Labour areas than in strong Conservative ones. The Labour Party share of the electorate, that is of those registered to vote, was only 30.9 per cent. Since 1945 only those governments which emerged after the two 1974 general elections secured the active support of a lower proportion of the electorate.

Competition amongst more than two parties continued:

- The Liberal Democrats won 46 seats, the largest number since 1929, twice as many as the Alliance secured in 1983 (see again Table 3). The third party's share of the votes cast declined slightly, by 1 per cent, for the third consecutive election, its second lowest share since 1974 (see again Table 4). However, it was still significantly higher than at any postwar election pre–1974.
- Parties other than the two major parties won 75 seats (see again Table 3), the highest since 1923. The share of the votes cast for candidates other than those from the three major parties was 9.3 per cent, the highest ever.
- The combined Labour–Conservative electoral strength was 74 per cent of the votes cast, lower than in the 1974 general elections (see again Table 4).

Soon after the 1997 General Election the Blair government set up a **joint Cabinet committee** involving ministers and senior Liberal Democrats, to discuss legislation both parties could support.

A multi-party system in Scotland

Competition amongst more than two parties at the first election to the Scottish Parliament reduced the chances of single–party government. The Labour Party won 56 seats, the SNP 35, the Conservative Party 18, the Liberal Democrats 17 and others 3. Donald Dewer, Leader of the Scottish Labour Party, and Jim Wallace, Leader of the Scottish Liberal Democrats, formed the first coalition government in Great Britain since 1945, with Dewer as First Minister and Wallace as Deputy First Minister.

The mechanism of cooperation and the policies the coalition would pursue were detailed in a 20–page document entitled *Partnership Scotland*. Two seats in the Cabinet and two junior ministerial positions were offered to the Liberal Democrats. The coalition document said that the relationship between the Scottish parliament and local government, 'including in particular the question of proportional representation', was being reviewed by the McIntosh commission. The Liberal Democrats had 'a long–standing commitment to proportional representation for elections to local government' and the coalition would ensure that publication of the final McIntosh recommendations were followed by 'an immediate programme of change, including progress on electoral reform.'

Wales

There was also competition amongst more than two parties at the first election to the Welsh Assembly in May 1999, with the Labour Party winning 28 seats, Plaid Cymru 17, the Conservative Party 9 and the Liberal Democrats 6. The Labour Party was able to rule alone, but not on the basis of a legislative majority.

The European Parliament

The first UK elections to be conducted under a system of proportional representation, to the European Parliament in June 1999, were also characterised by competition amongst more than two parties. The Conservative Party won 36 seats, the Labour Party 29, the Liberal Democrats 10, the United Kingdom Independence Party 3, the SNP 2, Plaid Cymru 2 and the Green Party 2. Parties other than the three major parties won 23 per cent of the votes cast, 19 per cent excluding the nationalists.

SUMMARY

A one–party system is one in which a single party enjoys a monopoly of power through the exclusion of all other parties (by political or constitutional means). A dominant–party system is a competitive party system dominated by a single major party that consequently enjoys a prolonged period of government power. A two–party system is one in which only two parties enjoy sufficient electoral and legislative strength to have a realistic prospect of winning government power; the larger party is able to rule alone; and power alternates between these parties. A multi–party system is characterised by competition amongst more than two parties reducing the chances of single–party government.

Party systems have implications for the political process in general, influencing the range and nature of choice available to the electorate, affecting the stability of governments, structuring the relationship between the executive and the legislature, establishing a bias in favour of either conflict and consensus and shaping the general character of the political culture.

The nature of the UK party system has changed from two–partyism, 1945–74, to multi–partyism, 1974–79, and dominant–partyism, 1979–97.

Revision hints

Make sure you have a comparative knowledge of different party systems and of their implications for the political process in general. You should have an understanding of the changing UK party system.

Exam hints

Answering stimulus questions on 'Party Systems'
Study the source material below and then answer question (a), (b) and (c).

GENERAL ELECTION	CONSERVATIVES		LABOUR		LIBERAL / ALLIANCE LIB. DEMOCRAT		OTHERS	
	% Votes	No. of seats	% Votes	No. of seats	% Votes	No. of seats	% Votes	No. of seats
1945	39.8	213	48.3	393	9.1	12	2.8	22
1950	43.5	299	46.1	315	9.1	9	1.3	2
1951	48.0	321	48.8	277	2.5	6	0.7	3
1995	49.7	345	46.4	277	2.7	6	1.2	2
1959	49.4	365	43.8	258	5.9	6	0.9	1
1964	43.4	304	44.1	317	11.2	9	1.3	–
1966	41.9	253	47.9	363	8.5	12	1.7	2
1970	46.4	330	43.0	287	7.5	6	3.1	7
Feb. 1974	37.8	297	37.1	301	19.3	14	5.8	23
Oct. 1974	35.8	277	39.2	319	18.3	13	6.7	26

GENERAL ELECTION	CONSERVATIVES		LABOUR		LIBERAL / ALLIANCE LIB. DEMOCRAT		OTHERS	
	% Votes	No. of seats	% Votes	No. of seats	% Votes	No. of seats	% Votes	No. of seats
1979	439	339	36.9	269	13.8	11	5.4	16
1983	42.4	397	27.6	209	25.4	23	4.6	21
1987	42.3	376	30.8	229	22.6	22	4.3	23
1992	41.9	336	34.4	271	17.8	20	5.9	24
1997	30.7	165	43.2	419	16.8	46	9.3	29

(a) From the data, illustrate ways in which the UK party system has changed in recent years.

(b) From the data, illustrate how significant features of the two–party system persist.

(c) Advance a case for the two–party system.

Answers to the above

(a) The data on the number of seats for the parties reveals a number of ways in which the UK party system has changed since the two–party system of the 1945–74 period, namely towards a multi–party system in the 1974–79 period and a dominant–party system in the 1979–97 period. The data on the percentages of votes cast for the parties highlights a long–term decline in Conservative–Labour electoral support and the electoral weakness of the modern Conservative Party. Use accurate and full evidence to support these points.

(b) However, the number of seats highlights how significant features of the two–party system persist in terms of Conservative and Labour domination of the House of Commons and, in 1997, the return of an alternation in power. Once again, support points by accurate evidence.

(c) This may include its capacity to offer voters a clear choice between likely parties of government, its capacity to ensure that the winning party is able to carry out its manifesto pledges, and its ability to tie government to the policies upon which they campaigned. Provide clear and full evidence in support of these points, from the UK and possibly elsewhere.

Practice questions

1 (a) Distinguish between a one-party system and a dominant-party system.
   (b) How does the definition of a dominant-party system run into problems.
2 Discuss the criteria for judging party systems.

4

IDEOLOGICAL TRADITIONS OF THE MAJOR PARTIES

Introduction

THIS CHAPTER WILL look at the ideologies, theories and traditions of the major UK parties. It will identify types of liberalism, conservatism and socialism.

Key Points

- Constitutionalism, Classical liberalism and New Liberalism.
- Toryism, One Nationism and the New Right.
- Socialism, social democracy and New Labour.

THE LIBERAL DEMOCRAT PARTY

'Any account of political ideologies must start with liberalism. This is because liberalism is, in effect, the ideology of the industrialised West' (Heywood, 1997). It is an ideology that is capable of embracing a broad range of rival values and beliefs.

Liberalism resulted from the breakdown of feudalism in Europe and the growth, in its place, of a market or capitalist society. In its earliest form, liberalism was a political doctrine. It reflected the aspirations of a rising middle class, attacking the absolute power of the monarchy and the privileges of the landed aristocracy. In place of absolutism it advocated constitutional and, later, representative government. As industrialisation spread throughout Western countries, liberal ideas and values shaped their political systems. These systems are constitutional in that they seek to limit government power and safeguard **civil liberties**, and

representative in the sense that political office is gained through competitive elections (see Simpson, 1998, pp. 31–3).

CONSTITUTIONALISM

Liberals see government as a necessary evil, necessary to uphold public order, but always liable to become a tyranny against the individual. They believe that the experience of political power is itself corrupting, encouraging those who possess it to abuse it at the expense of others. This was expressed in the famous words of Lord Acton, 'Power tends to corrupt and absolute power corrupts absolutely'. As a result, liberals believe in the principle of limited government. This has traditionally taken the form of constitutionalism, a system of government according to prescribed rules which imposes limits on the government.

In practice, government can be limited in two ways. In the first place, it can be limited by external constraints upon what government can do. For example, a 'written' or codified constitution sets significant limits to the exercise of government power when its provisions are justiciable, that is enforceable by the courts; the protection of the rights of individuals can be entrenched in a bill of rights providing a legal definition of the rights of individuals in the relationships between them and the state. Secondly, government can be limited by internal constraints which break up or fragment government power, creating checks and balances. For example, the decentralisation of government power, achieved most radically by federalism, in which sovereignty is divided between two levels of government, promotes fragmentation.

Liberal ideology is characterised by a commitment to individualism, a belief in the supreme importance of the human individual as opposed to any social group or collective body. This leads naturally to a commitment to individual freedom. Individual freedom, or liberty is 'the core value of liberal ideology' (Heywood, 1997). Liberals believe that individuals are entitled to the widest possible liberty consistent with a like liberty for all.

CLASSICAL LIBERALISM

The earliest liberal tradition was classical liberalism. It developed during the transition from feudalism to capitalism, and reached its high point in the early nineteenth century. Classical liberalism is characterised by a belief in negative freedom, that is the absence of external constraints upon the individual, or non-interference. It is distinguished by a belief in a minimal state, acting merely as a nightwatchman, its role limited to the protection of individuals from each other.

As an economic theory, classical liberalism believes in the free market as a mechanism tending to deliver general prosperity and opportunities for all. The market should be free from government interference because it is managed by what Adam Smith referred to, in *The Wealth of Nations* (1776), as 'an invisible hand'. Free market beliefs reached their high point with the doctrine of *laissez-faire*, meaning literally 'to leave to do'. This is the idea that the economy does best when left alone by government.

NEW LIBERALISM

John Stuart Mill provided a 'bridge' between classical liberalism and New Liberalism, his ideas looking backwards to the early nineteenth century and forward to the twentieth century. The ideas developed in 'On Liberty' (1859) portrayed freedom as the absence of all restrictions upon an individual's 'self-regarding' actions, a conception of liberty which is essentially 'negative'. Mill believed this to be a necessary, but not in itself a sufficient, condition for liberty. He was concerned with personal self-development. 'As such, he laid the foundation for a positive theory of liberty' (Heywood, 1998a).

The clearest break with classical liberalism cam with the work of **T.H. Green** in the late nineteenth century. Negative freedom had merely given individuals 'freedom to' think and act as they please, while positive freedom involved gaining 'freedom from' social evils such as poverty, sickness, unemployment and ignorance.

New Liberals of the early twentieth century, such as **L.T. Hobhouse**, were committed to intervention by the state. He declared: 'There is no intrinsic and inevitable conflict between liberty and compulsion, but at bottom a mutual need. The object of compulsion is to secure the most favourable external conditions of inward growth and happiness so far as these conditions depend on combined action and uniform observance' (Hobhouse).

"we need to restate the views of the turn-of-the-century New Liberals such as L.T. Hobhouse who was among the first people in Britain to recognise that 'the struggle for liberty is.... a struggle for equality'. For all to be free argued Hobhouse, there had to be equal access to opportunities for education and employment, and only individuals together, acting through government, could ensure such equality of opportunity. Today, we ignore this view at our peril".

(Charles Kennedy, successful candidate for the Liberal Democrat leadership, 'Escape into freedom', *The Guardian*, 5 August 1999)

The Beveridge Report, 1942, a blueprint for the welfare state, was provided b y a twentieth century Liberal, William Beveridge. It advocated positive freedom, from five giant evils: Want, Disease, Ignorance, Squalor and Idleness. The 1944 White Paper on Employment Policy, in which the government accepted as one of its primary aims and responsibilities 'the maintenance of a high and stable level of employment,' was largely due to the work of another twentieth century Liberal, John Maynard Keynes. In *The General Theory of Employment, Interest and*

Money (1936), he challenged classical economic theory and rejected its idea of a self-regulating market. Keynes developed the theory of demand management, that is management of the total level of demand in the economy by the government through its tax and spending policies. At times of high unemployment, government should manage demand by cutting taxes or increasing public spending.

THE CONSERVATIVE PARTY

The origins of the Conservative Party could be traced back to the Tories who opposed the Revolutionary settlement of 1688–89. 'No doubt it can be argued', writes Blake, 'that there is some sort of continuity of ideas — a Tory attitude to political problems — which can be traced back through the eighteenth century to the political struggles in the reign of Charles II'. The word Tory was first used as a term of abuse for Catholic outlaws and was applied to those who supported the legitimate heir to the throne in spite of his adherence to the Roman Catholic Church.

TORYISM

Heywood (1997) defines Toryism as 'an ideological stance within conservatism characterised by a belief in hierarchy, an emphasis on tradition, and support for duty and organicism'.

- *Hierarchy*: Tories believe that gradations of social position and status are natural and inevitable.
- *Tradition*: Tories emphasis tradition because it reflects the accumulated wisdom of the past. The institutions and practices that have been 'tested by time' should be preserved for the benefit of the living and for generations to come. Tradition also gives the individual a sense of belonging, thus promoting stability.
- *Duty*: They support duty, viewing society as bound together by mutual obligations and reciprocal duties.
- *Organicism*: They support the view that society is an organic whole, or living entity, the whole being more than a collection of its individual parts. Society thus arises out of natural necessity. Its various institutions, such as the family and the nation, contribute to the stability of society.

ONE NATIONISM

Conservatism as a distinctive political ideology first emerged in the late eighteenth and early nineteenth centuries. It arose as a reaction against the growing pace of economic and political change, which was in many ways symbolised by the French Revolution. One of the earliest statements of conservative principles is contained in Edmund Burke's *Reflections on the Revolution in France* (1790) which deeply regretted the revolutionary challenge to the *ancien regime*, that is the old order. In trying to resist the pressures unleashed by the growth of liberalism, socialism and nationalism, conservatism stood in defence of an increasingly embattled traditional social order. However, Burke advocated, not blind resistance to change, but a prudent willingness to 'change in order to conserve'. This stance enabled conservatism in the nineteenth century to embrace 'One Nationism'.

The One Nation tradition can be traced back to the early writings of Benjamin Disraeli, before he became Prime Minister (1868, 1874–80). In his novel, *Sybil, or, The two nations* (1845), he warned of the danger of Britain being divided into two nations, the rich and the poor. In true conservative tradition, his ideas were based upon 'a combination of prudence and principle' (Heywood, 1998a). Growing inequality contained the seed of revolution. Reform would be prudent because, in stemming revolution, it would ultimately be in the interests of the rich. Disraeli also appealed to the principle of duty. This was based upon neo-feudal ideas such as *noblesse oblige*, that is the obligations of the nobility. Wealth and privilege brought with them social obligations, in particular a responsibility to look after the poor. This was, in effect, the price of privilege. These ideas provide the basis of what is called One Nation conservatism, 'the cornerstone of what can properly be termed a Tory position' (Heywood, 1997), 'entirely consistent with principles such as organicism, hierarchy and duty' (Ibid).

One Nationism has not only been prepared to accept that government should provide social welfare, but also that economic policy should not simply be left to the market. In *The Middle Way*, 1938, Harold Macmillan, later to be Conservative Prime Minister, 1957–63, advocated what he called 'planned capitalism', which he described as 'a mixed system which combines state ownership, regulation or control of certain aspects of economic activity with the drive and initiative of private enterprise' (Macmillan, 1966). Macmillan was, at the time, MP for Stockton, an area seriously affected by unemployment, and he possessed the privileged social background and sense of obligation associated with One Nationism.

The high point of the One Nation tradition came in the 1950s as the Conservative Party adapted to the post–war political consensus of the managed economy and the welfare state (see Chapter 5).

THE NEW RIGHT

The phrase which best summarises the ideas of the New Right is 'the free economy and the strong state'. What sets the New Right apart is the combination of neo-liberalism, 'a traditional liberal defence of the free economy', and neo-conservatism, 'a traditional conservative defence of state authority'. (Gamble, 1988).

Neo-Liberalism

The liberal tendency is drawn from classical liberalism. It is an updated version of the free market ideas of economists such as Adam Smith developed in the writings of Friedrich Hayek and Milton Friedman. The liberal conception of a free economy denotes 'a spontaneous harmony of interests generated through the voluntary exchanges of free autonomous individuals within a framework of agreed rules' (Gamble, 1988). To safeguard the order which the market spontaneously generates a state is needed, but a state minimal in its functions and limited in its powers. However, although the state is to be limited it needs to be strong in carrying out its functions. Policing the market order requires vigilance and firm action to enforce laws impartially so that competition is fair, exchange voluntary, and the fruits of enterprise secure.

Neo-conservatism

Conservatives 'see the state as end and not as means' (Roger Scruton, 1980)... 'its substance is power, and its form authority'. As Scruton puts it, 'Society exists through authority, and the recognition of this authority requires the allegiance to a bond that is not contractual but transcendent, in the manner of the family tie. Such allegiance requires tradition and custom through which to find enactment. A conservative 'will seek to uphold all those practices and institutions — among which, of course, the family is pre-eminent — through which the habits of allegiance are acquired'. Changes in the laws 'which are calculated to loosen or abolish the obligations of family life, or which in other ways facilitate the channelling of libidinal impulse away from that particular form of union, will be accepted by the conservative only under the pressure of necessity'.

It may be 'no part of conservatism to be associated with any particular economic policy' (Scruton, 1980). It came to seem as though 'a Hayek or a Freidman could speak about political matters with the authority of a scientist, when in fact his political dogma remained detachable from his economic theory, the theory itself being as scientifically unadventurous and as empirically arbitrary as any of its competitors'. The connection with the free economy arises because 'the need for private property stems automatically from the basic attitude of conservatism'. The principle of a conservative's outlook is a person's 'absolute and ineradicable need of private property'. Private property is added to, and reinforces 'the primary social bond'. It is for some such reason that conservatives have seen the family and private property as 'institutions which stand or fall together'.

Thatcherism

New Right ideas were articulated in the 1980s in the form of Thatcherism. Margaret Thatcher, Conservative Prime Minister 1979–90, famously commented that 'there is no such thing as society ... there are individual men and women, and there are families'.

William Hague

William Hague, Leader of the Conservative Party after its disastrous defeat in the 1997 General Election, seemed to be moving away from Thatcherism. In his campaign for the leadership he said that the party needed a 'fresh start' and a month later, on 23 July 1997, he spelt out how to turn that fresh start into a 'fresh future'. He defined the task as first listening to people, second giving a genuine welcome to new ideas and third adjusting to the ideas and the psychology of the new century. In a speech to the think-tank Politeia on 27 July 1995 Hague said he did believe that 'there is such a thing as society'.

However, Conservative Party strategists said the package of policies contained in the document, *The Common Sense Revolution*, published at the time of the Conservative Party Conference in October 1999, marked a 'return to Thatcherism' ("Hague's 'revolution' harks back to Thatcher," Andrew Grice, *The Independent*, 5 October, 1999). Andrew Lansley, Conservative shadow cabinet member with responsibility for policy renewal, claimed that the Conservative Party was 'historically and today, a party born of three traditions'. They were: 'Toryism, in defence of our constitution and way of life'; 'One Nation' Conservatism, 'recognising the need for the advantages of economic and social progress to be shared by the whole people, in order to avoid social division; and 'classical liberalism', using the power of free markets to create wealth and opportunity. All three of these values, he added, were 'represented in our common sense revolution'. ('We need a common sense revolution', *The Independent*, 4/10/99).

THE CONSERVATIVE PARTY AND EUROPE

The Conservative governments of Macmillan and Heath applied to join the Common Market, or European Economic Community, for essentially economic rather than political reasons. It was anticipated that membership would open up a large new home market for British goods and services. The removal of barriers to internal trade within Europe fitted comfortably within the free market ideas associated with the New Right. Thatcher signed the Single European Act in 1985.

However, aspects of the European Community increasingly appeared to the New Right to be less consistent with their free market principles and more reminiscent of corporatism. In particular, the 'social dimension' of the Community was seen as a threat to the 'free economy'. In September 1988 Thatcher said, in her speech in Bruges, she had not spent nine years rolling back the frontiers of the state at home only to see them rolled forward by Brussels. Thatcher's successor, Major, sought and obtained an opt-out from the Social Chapter of the 1991 Maastricht Treaty.

Statist tendencies do not alone explain the Conservative Party attitude to Europe. The New Right was, as we have seen (page 31), about more than free markets, drawing also on the neo-conservative wish to uphold state authority. It became increasingly concerned about what it saw as the political agenda of the European Union, Eurofederalism, and the threat this was perceived to pose to national sovereignty. The Conservative government's belated entry into the Exchange Rate Mechanism in 1990 and its ignominious forced departure on 'Black Wednesday', 16 September 1992, increased antagonism to the whole European project and turned the prospect of a single European currency into an issue on which the New Right was determined to make a stand.

Major conceded a referendum on the issue and otherwise adopted a 'wait and see' approach. Within weeks of the Conservative Party Conference in 1997, Hague moved to a firm pledge which ruled out joining the single currency for the current Parliament and the next, effectively for ten years. In the European elections, June 1999, the Conservative Party said that it wanted Britain to be in Europe, but not run by Europe. Hague made the single currency a key issue in his campaign. In his speech to the 1999 Conservative Party Conference on 7 October Hague said it must make sense, 'not to drive for ever closer political union but to create a flexible and open European Union of nation states'. When in government 'the next new EU Treaty must contain a flexibility clause or else I tell you there will be no new Treaty'.

THE CONSERVATIVE PARTY AND THE CONSTITUTION

The preservation of national sovereignty has not only involved the Conservative Party resisting external threats to the integrity and independence of the UK but also opposing measures which are seen to threaten the Union from the inside. In response to the conversion of Gladstone's Liberal Party to Home Rule for Ireland, the Conservative Party became, in the late nineteenth century, the champions of the Union, even changing the name of the party to the Conservative and Unionist Party. A Conservative-dominated coalition under the Liberal Lloyd George was obliged to concede independence to what was to become the Republic of Ireland, and Home Rule for the remaining six counties of Northern Ireland. More recent Conservative governments have been forced to contemplate more radical solutions for the island of Ireland. Effectively, concern for the Union has been transferred from Ireland to Great Britain, and to the future of Scotland and Wales in particular. Both Thatcher and Major strongly opposed devolution to Scotland and Wales. Hague campaigned for a 'No' vote in the devolution referendums in Scotland and Wales.

THE LABOUR PARTY

SOCIALISM

Although Socialist ideas can be traced back to the Levellers and the Diggers of the seventeenth century, or to Thomas More's *Utopia* (1516), or even Plato's *Republic*, socialism developed in the nineteenth century as a reaction against the economic and social conditions generated in Europe by the emergence of industrial capitalism. It was closely linked to the development of a new but growing industrial working class. Heywood (1997) defines socialism as 'an ideology characterised by a belief in community, cooperation, equality and common ownership'.

- *Community*: 'The core of socialism is the vision of human beings as social creatures' (Heywood, 1997), capable of overcoming economic and social problems by drawing upon the power of the community rather than individual effort. This is a collectivist vision because it stresses the capacity of human beings for collective action, their willingness and ability to pursue goals by working together, as opposed to striving for personal self–interest.
- *Cooperation*: If human beings are social animals, socialists believe that the natural relationship amongst them is one of cooperation rather than competition. Cooperation strengthens the bonds of community and harnesses the energies of the community rather than those of the individual, while competition pits individuals against each other.
- *Equality*: Equality has been defined as 'the central value of socialism' (Heywood, 1997). Socialists emphasise the importance of social equality, an equality of outcome as opposed to equality of opportunity.
- *Common ownership*: The socialist case for common ownership is that it is a means of harnessing material resources to the common good, with private property promoting selfishness, breeding acquisitiveness and being divisive. The Labour Party, according to Clause IV of its constitution, adopted in 1918, had a formal commitment:

'To secure for the workers by hand or by brain the full fruits of their industry and the most equitable distribution thereof that may be possible upon the basis of the common ownership of the means of production, distribution and exchange, and the best obtainable system of popular administration and control of each industry or service'.

SOCIAL DEMOCRACY

Social democracy 'stands for a balance between the market and the state' (Heywood, 1997).

Revisionism

Social democracy revised socialism. Socialism, in the view of revisionists, was 'basically about equality' (Tony Crosland, 1956). By equality, they meant more than equality of opportunity, as the greatest rewards would go to those with the most fortunate genetic endowment and family background. They adopted the 'strong' definition of equality, what Rawls (1958) subsequently called the 'democratic' as opposed to the 'liberal' conception, a conception which Crosland endorsed in *Socialism Now* (1974). Revisionists wanted also a "redistribution of income ... a wider social equality embracing also the distribution of property, the educational system, social-class relationships, power and privilege in industry — indeed all that was enshrined in the age-old socialist dream of a more 'classless society'" (Crosland, 1974).

Revisionism was a thesis about means as well as ends. It maintained, contrary to traditional Marxist doctrine, that 'the ownership of the means of production had ceased to be the key factor which imparts to a society its essential character' (Crosland, 1956). It was therefore possible to achieve the goal of greater equality within the framework of a mixed economy, with public ownership taking its place as only one of a number of possible means for attaining the end in view.

Social democracy was thus associated with a desire to reform or 'humanise' capitalism through state intervention.

- The mixed economy, a blend of public and private ownership, would help government to regulate economic activity.
- Keynesian demand management would maintain high employment and guarantee economic growth.
- Welfare provision funded via progressive taxation would redistribute from the rich to the poor.

However, recession in the mid–1970s simultaneously expanded welfare spending as unemployment grew, and squeezed the tax revenues which finance welfare spending, because fewer people were at work and businesses were less profitable. The growth of globalisation has rendered invalid social democratic assumptions about the nature of capitalism, particularly the capacity of national governments to manage demand. National economic policy has to focus more on supply–side measures, such as promoting long–term investment and education. De–industrialisation, that is the decline of manufacturing industry, led to class de–alignment. When most voters were working–class, democracy and social democracy went hand in hand. The emergence in modern societies of a 'contented majority' (Galbraith, 1992) provided an electoral base for tax cuts rather than welfare spending.

NEW LABOUR

According to Anthony Giddens (1998), 'the first systematic attempt to move away from classical social democratic principles was contained in the Labour Party Policy Review', set up under the leadership of Neil Kinnock in response to the party's third successive election defeat in 1987. Particular emphasis in the policy review proposals, *Meet the Challenge Make the Change* (1989), was placed upon supply side intervention, investment being promised in training, education and technology.

Blair completed the transition to what came to be called 'New Labour' with the symbolically significant revision of Clause IV of the Labour Party constitution. For Philip Gould the 'brainstorming' day at the Chewton Glen Hotel in Hampshire on 9 September 1994 was memorable for 'one defining moment'. In the queue with Blair, waiting for the buffet, Blair and Gould talked about the need for rapid change. Blair turned to Gould and made 'one of the most compelling political statements' Gould had ever heard: 'Conference must build New Labour. It is time we gave the party some electric shock treatment' (Gould, 1998). The slogan 'New Labour, New Britain' was used at the Labour Party Conference later that month. Toward the end of his speech at the conference Blair made reference to changing the constitution of the party. An alternative to Clause IV was approved at a special party conference in 1995:

'The Labour Party is a democratic socialist party. It believes that by the strength of our common endeavour we achieve more than we achieve alone, so as to create for each of us the means to realise our true potential and for all of us a community in which power, wealth and opportunity are in the hands of the many, not the few, where the rights we enjoy reflect the duties we owe, and where we live together, freely, in a spirit of solidarity, tolerance and respect'.

The ideological character of New Labour has been described as 'one of the most difficult' issues in modern British politics (Heywood, 1998b).

Communitarianism

'Communitarianism is the belief that the community is the source of the individual's identity and values, and, as such, that the individual owes the community a debt of loyalty and consideration' (Heywood, 1998b). Communitarian ideas can be traced back to nineteenth–century anarchist ideas about unregulated social harmony based upon human sociability, but their modern version, associated with theorists such as MacIntyre and Sandel, emerged as a critique of liberal individualism. They have argued that, in conceiving of the individual as logically prior to and 'outside' the community, liberalism has merely legitimised selfish and egotistical behaviour, downgrading the importance of the idea of the public good. In their view there is no such thing as an unencumbered self; the self is always constituted through the community.

Communitarianism has been popularised by theorists such as Etzioni in the USA, who influenced the Clinton Democrat administration.

In the UK, a liberal version of communitarianism has been advanced by John Gray, a writer once associated with the New Right. 'The emblematic theme of liberal communitarianism is the idea of moral responsibility... a view of the individual as a self-willed and accountable actor supported by a strong public culture' (Heywood, 1998b). In emphasising cultural solutions to social breakdown rather than economic ones, it has in effect replaced social engineering with cultural engineering.

However, communitarianism 'deradicalises the thrust of socialist theory', which can be seen in its tendency 'to highlight the ties that bind all members of society and thus to ignore or conceal class differences and economic inequalities' (Heywood, 1998a). It represents 'a shift towards authority and away from individual liberty' (Heywood, 1997), in its emphasis on moral responsibility. Communitarianism has 'conservative implications as it tends to be associated with attempts to strengthen existing institutions such as the family' (Heywood, 1998a), instead of with the task of social transformation.

Stakeholding

Another idea which seemed for a time destined to embody the essence of New Labour doctrine was stakeholding. Championed by Will Hutton, it seeks to offer an alternative to 'shareholder capitalism' that is based upon the idea of social partnership as practised by Germany and other parts of continental Europe. According to Gould, stakeholding was a first attempt at synthesising society and efficiency. David Miliband, Blair's head of policy, came up with a 'stakeholder Britain that combines one–nation society with one–nation economics' (Gould, 1998). Blair made his stakeholder speech in Singapore on 8 January 1996, linking society to efficiency: 'We need a new relationship of trust not just within a firm but within society. By trust I mean the recognition of a mutual purpose for which we work together and in which we all benefit. It is a stakeholder economy in which opportunity is available to all, advancement is through merit and from which no group or class is set apart or excluded. This is the economic justification for social cohesion, for a fair and strong society'. The night before Blair's stakeholder speech Alastair Campbell, Press Secretary to Blair, contacted two local journalists from *The Telegraph* and *The Guardian* who were there and briefed them on the speech, telling them 'this was the big idea' (Gould, 1998). This speech 'immediately gave New Labour its defining idea'.

However, it ran into difficulty just as quickly. It was 'open to attack as being corporatist, just when corporatist solutions appeared to be failing in Europe and non–corporatist Asian tigers were starting to roar'. Gordon Brown, Shadow Chancellor of the Exchequer, did not like stakeholding as an economic idea. He felt it was a hostage to fortune, exposing New Labour to the risk of attack on grounds of social costs. The most difficult decision of some last–minute rewriting of the policy document, *'New Life for Britain'*, by Peter Mandelson (Director of Campaigns and Communications), David Miliband and Philip Gould, the night before its launch on 4 July 1996, was whether or not to include stakeholding as a section heading. Stakeholding had fallen out of fashion somewhat, but for reasons of continuity they 'felt it better to keep it in'. The idea of stakeholding was quickly abandoned once Blair took office. Labour in power looked more favourably upon the model of US–style 'enterprise' capitalism than upon German–style 'social market' capitalism.

The Third Way

As Giddens (1998) explains, the term 'third way' is 'of no particular significance in and of itself'. It has been used many times before in the past history of social democracy, and also by writers and politicians of quite different political persuasions. Giddens makes use of it in his book, *The Third Way*, to refer to 'social democratic renewal' (Giddens, 1998).

Frequently referred to as Blair's guru, Giddens says that third way politics should preserve a core concern with social justice. Equality and individual freedom may conflict, but egalitarian measures also often increase the range of freedoms open to individuals. Freedom 'should mean autonomy of action, which in turn demands the involvement of the wider social community'.

He suggests as a prime motto for the Third Way, *no rights without responsibilities*. Government has a whole cluster of responsibilities for its citizens and others, including the 'protection of the vulnerable'. However, social democracy was inclined to treat rights as unconditional claims. With expanding individualism should come an 'extension of individual obligations'. For example, unemployment benefits should carry the obligation to look actively for work. It is highly important that, as an ethical principle, 'no rights without responsibilities' must apply not only to welfare recipients, but to everyone, because otherwise the precept can be held to apply only to the poor or the needy.

Third way values

Equality
Protection of the vulnerable
Freedom as autonomy
No rights without responsibilities
No authority without democracy
Cosmopolitan pluralism
Philosophic conservation

SOURCE: Giddens, *The Third Way*, 1998

A second precept should be *no authority without democracy*. In a society where tradition and custom are losing their hold, the only route to the establishing of authority is via democracy. It must be recast on an active or participatory basis.

Other issues include responses to globalisation, scientific and technological change, and our relationship to the natural world. In response to the questions about how to recreate social solidarity and how to react to ecological problems, strong emphasis has to be given to 'cosmopolitan values', and to what might be called 'philosophical conservatism'. A cosmopolitan outlook is the necessary condition of a multicultural society in a globalising order. The theme of philosophic conservation is central to the need to re–establish continuity and develop social cohesion in a world of erratic transformation, where he intrinsically unpredictable energies of scientific and technological innovation play such an important role. 'Conservatism' in this sense suggests a pragmatic attitude towards coping with change; a nuanced view of science and technology, in recognition of their ambiguous consequences for us; a respect for the past and for history; and in the environmental area, an adoption of the precautionary principle where feasible.

Giddens defines equality as *inclusion*. Inclusion refers in its broadest sense to citizenship, to 'the civil and political rights and obligations that all members of a society should have, not just formally, but as a reality of their lives'. It also refers to 'opportunities and to involvement in public space'. For example, in a society where work remains central to self–esteem and standard of living access to work is one main context of opportunity. Education is another.

Blair said, in *The Third Way: New Politics for the New Century* (1998), that the Third Way 'stands for a modernised social democracy, passionate in its commitment to social justice, ... but flexible, innovative and forward-looking in the means to achieve it'. It is founded on the values of 'democracy, liberty, justice, mutual obligation and internationalism'. However, 'it is a *third* way because it moves decisively beyond an Old Left preoccupied by state control, high taxation and producer interests', and a New Right 'treating public investment ... and collective endeavour, as evils to be undone'.

The Third Way is 'not an attempt to split the difference between Right and Left'. It is 'about traditional values in a changed world', and draws vitality from uniting democratic socialism and liberalism. Liberals asserted the primacy of individual liberty in the market economy, social democrats promoted social justice with the state as its main agent. There is no necessary conflict between the two, accepting now that state power is one means to achieve their goals, but not the only one and emphatically not an end in itself. (Blair, p. 1, *The Third Way*, 1998).

Four values are essential to a just society – **equal worth, opportunity for all, responsibility and community.**

- Social justice must be founded on 'the equal worth of each individual, whatever their background, capability, creed or race'.
- The constitution of the Labour Party commits it to seek the widest possible spread of wealth, power and opportunity. Blair highlighted opportunity as a key value. For most people, opportunities are inseparable from society, in which government action necessarily plays a large part. Gross inequalities continue to be handed down from generation to generation, and the Third Way must 'robustly tackle the obstacles to true equality of opportunity'. It does not take a narrow view of opportunities: the arts and the creative industries should be part of our common culture.
- For too long, the demand for rights from the state was separated from the duties of citizenship and the imperative for mutual responsibility on the part of individuals and institutions. For example, unemployment benefits were often paid without strong reciprocal obligations, children went unsupported by absent parents. This issue persists. For example, our responsibility to protect the environment is increasingly pressing, so is the responsibility of parents for their children's education. The 'rights we enjoy reflect the duties we owe; rights and opportunity without responsibility are engines of selfishness and greed'.
- Human nature is cooperative as well as competitive, selfless as well as self–interested. Society could not function if it was otherwise. We all depend on collective goods for our independence. All our lives are enriched — or impoverished — by the communities to which we belong. In deciding where to act on behalf of the national community, whether as regulator or provider, governments must be acutely sensitive not to stifle worthwhile activity by local communities and the voluntary sector. Freedom for the many requires strong government. A key challenge is 'to use the state as an enabling force, protecting effective communities and voluntary organisations and encouraging their growth to tackle new needs, in partnership as appropriate' (Blair, 1998).

Blair concluded that the Third Way is 'a modernised social democracy for a changing world'.

However, it is debatable whether the Third Way is ideologically meaningful or coherent. Asked what was the Third Way, one new Labour MP replied: 'The Third Way is in the eye of the beholder' (private conversation with author, 1999).

NEW LABOUR, THE ECONOMY AND PUBLIC SERVICES

- In the words of the new Clause IV, New Labour works for 'a dynamic economy', in which 'the enterprise of the market and the rigour of competition' are joined with the forces of partnership and co–operation to produce the wealth the nation needs, with 'a thriving private sector' and high quality public services. This is a different mix of private and public than the mixed economy of social democracy.

- The economic strategy of New Labour is 'firmly post-Keynesian'. New Labour believes in a 'a neo–liberal economic philosophy committed to tight limits on public spending, low inflation, low levels of direct taxation, labour flexibility and trade liberalisation' (Heywood, 1998b).
- In the public services, New Labour demands that rights must be balanced against responsibilities. For example, the welfare–to–work strategy, to ensure that more people come off benefit, or receive benefits as part of being in work, is in its view 'the best way of moving people out of poverty and ensuring that individuals discharge the duties of citizenship' (Plant, 1999). Parents are encouraged and even enforced 'to bring up children as competent, responsible citizens, and to support those — such as teachers — who are employed by the state in the task', as with initiatives such as 'home-school contacts' between schools and parents (Blair, 1998).

The transition of the Labour Party from a socialist to a post-socialist party was marked, if not before, in the joint document of the Labour Party and the German Social Democrats, *Europe: The Third Way* (1999), which stated: 'The promotion of social justice was sometimes confused with the imposition of equality of outcome'.

THE LABOUR PARTY AND EUROPE

In 1962, the Labour Party leader, Hugh Gaitskell, came out decisively against entry to the European Community. Although his successor, Wilson, was subsequently converted to membership, by 1983 the Labour Party was actually committed to a British withdrawal from the Community without even a referendum. The Community was seen as a capitalist club which would impede the development of socialist policies in the UK.

However, since then the Labour Party has not only become reconciled to membership of the European Union , but positively enthusiastic. The Blair government signed up to the Social Charter of the Maastricht Treaty, which was compatible with its own ideas on social policy, including the minimum wage.

NEW LABOUR AND THE CONSTITUTION

The Blair government's constitutional reforms since 1997 constitute 'the most far-reaching and coherent programme of constitutional reform attempted by any government in the twentieth century' (Heywood, 1998b). They included devolution to Scotland and Wales, the incorporation of the European Convention on Human Rights into UK law, a freedom of information act, reform of the House of Lords and the possibility of electoral reform for the House of Commons.

Constitutional radicalism fits into New Labour ideology in the following ways:

- It reflects Giddens' Third Way value that authority must be recast on an active or participatory basis (see pages 39–41).

- A party no longer committed to radical socialist reform does not need concentrated constitutional power.
- Of 'perhaps the greatest long–term significance', it 'may provide a basis for a realignment of the party system by bringing about a closer and enduring relationship between the Labour Party and the Liberal Democrats' (Heywood, 1998b). Blair said in his first speech to the Labour Party Conference as Prime Minister in 1997: 'Division among radicals almost 100 years ago resulted in a twentieth century dominated by Conservatives. I want the twenty-first century to be the century of the radicals'. His unprecedented initiative in bringing the Liberal Democrats onto a Cabinet committee was clearly not a response to any immediate electoral necessity. It could be understood 'only as a move in a larger strategy the aim of which is the reinvention of liberal Britain' (John Gray, 'Tories on the brink', *The Guardian*, 22 September, 1997).

However, the Human Rights Act, 1998, which incorporates the European Convention on Human Rights into UK law, denies the courts the power to strike down Acts of Parliament. The Scotland Act, 1998, which established a Scottish Parliament with legislative power, limits Scotland to varying the basic rate of income tax by plus or minus threepence; the Government of Wales Act, 1998, which established a Welsh Assembly with powers of secondary legislation only, gives Wales no tax raising powers at all (see Hazell, 1999).

SUMMARY

Liberalism emerged as a political doctrine committed to the establishment of constitutionalism. In its classical form, liberalism is distinguished by a belief in a minimal state, whose role is limited to the protection of individuals from each other. As an economic theory, classical liberalism believes in the free market as a mechanism tending to deliver general prosperity and opportunities for all. New Liberalism is characterised by a more sympathetic attitude towards intervention by the state.

Toryism is an ideological stance within conservatism which is characterised by a belief in hierarchy, an emphasis upon tradition and support for duty and organicism. One Nationism is based on neofeudal ideas such as *noblesse oblige*, the cornerstone of what can properly be termed a Tory position, entirely consistent with principles such as organicism, hierarchy and duty. The ideas of the New Right are best summarised as the free economy and the strong state, the combination of neo–liberalism, a traditional liberal defence of the free economy, and neo–conservatism, a traditional conservative defence of state authority.

Socialism is an ideology characterised by a belief in community, cooperation, equality and common ownership. Social democracy stands for a balance between the market and the state. New Labour marks the transition of the Labour Party from a socialist to a post-socialist party.

STUDY GUIDE

Revision hints

Make sure you know the ideologies, theories and traditions of the major UK parties. You should be able to identify types of liberalism, conservatism and socialism.

Exam hints

Answering structure essay questions on 'Ideological Traditions of the Major Parties'

1 Question 1(c) in Chapter 2 can be answered from material contained in this Chapter.

    Identify the main points of disagreement between the major UK parties, such as Europe and constitutional reform, giving attention to the distinctive theories, ideologies and policies of each party.

Answering essay questions on 'Ideological Traditions of the Major Parties'

2 Can the modern Labour Party still be regarded as a socialist party? (Specimen Papers with Mark Schemes, Edexcel GCE Government and Politics, Unit Test 6B – Ideological Developments in the UK, Advanced, 2000 Edexcel).

Analyse ideological developments within the Labour Party. Examine the nature of socialism and link it to core values such as community, co-operation and equality, with Labour Party socialism taking the form of Keynesian social democracy, the desire to reform capitalism through strategic economic and social intervention. Examine the 'Blair project' and 'new' Labour in terms of their significance for socialism. In particular, discuss the shift in emphasis from a mixed economy, welfare and redistribution to responsibility, enterprise and constitutionalism, together with the idea of a viable 'third way' between social democracy and Thatcherism.

Practice questions

1 Assess the changing character of British conservatism.
2 Explain the impact of liberal ideology upon the theories and ideas of the major political parties.

5

POLICIES OF THE MAJOR PARTIES

Introduction

THIS CHAPTER WILL look at the policies, programmes and manifestos of the major political parties. It will include changing party images, consulting wider opinion, involvement of non–party members.

Key Points
- Policies, programmes and manifestos of the major political parties.
- Changing party images.
- Consulting wider opinion.
- Involvement of non–party members.

POLICIES, PROGRAMMES AND MANIFESTOS

THE POST–WAR POLITICAL CONSENSUS

The package of policies on the domestic front of what has been called the post–war political consensus included: full employment as a goal of economic policy; a mix of public and private ownership of industries and services; an active role for government; state provision of welfare; and conciliation of the trade unions. (Kavanagh, 1997).

There was interdependence in this package of policies. For example, the ideas of Keynes legitimised a large public sector, active government and welfare expenditure, also enhancing the bargaining position of trade unions; the ideas of Beveridge also legitimised a large public sector and active government, as well as conciliating the trade unions; the trade unions favoured full employment, public ownership and welfare.

Full Employment

The conscious pursuit of full employment as a goal of economic policy was first expressed in the war–time coalition government White Paper on *Employment Policy* (HMSO, 1944). In this the government accepted 'as one of the primary aims and responsibilities the maintenance of a high and stable level of employment after the war'. In line with Keynesian ideas, the goal of producing full employment by managing demand was gradually accepted by all parties. By 1950 the manifesto of the Conservative Party for the general election of that year stated: 'We regard the achievement of full employment as the first aim of a Conservative Government'. Between 1948 and 1970 the annual average level of unemployment never exceeded 3 per cent, compared with the norm of 10 per cent during the inter–war years. When unemployment threatened to reach 1 million in 1972 the Heath Conservative government expanded the money supply and reflated the economy through greater public spending.

A Mixed Economy

The manifesto of the Labour Party for the General Election of 1945 said that there were 'basic industries ripe and over-ripe for public ownership' and 'many smaller businesses rendering good service' which could be 'left to get on with their useful work'. (*Let Us Face The Future*, The Labour Party, 1945). It submitted to the nation a programme of public ownership of the fuel and power industries, inland transport, iron and steel. Most nationalisation measures involved the state taking over industries, reorganising them, and providing investment. The Labour Party justified its measures on pragmatic rather than ideological grounds. In *Public Ownership: The Next Step* (1948), it laid down five conditions which would make an industry suitable for nationalisation: inefficiency, for example poor management or low investment; bad industrial relations; monopoly position; need for investment of capital on a large scale; and being a major supplier of raw materials. The industries were established as statutory monopolies, run as public corporations, and instructed to 'break even' taking one year with another, rather than make profits. There was little that was distinctively socialist about the programme.

Although the Conservative Party was committed to private ownership, it had already established public corporations before the war. The 1924–9 Baldwin government set up the British Broadcasting Corporation (BBC) and the Central Electricity Generating Board. In the 1930s the Conservative-dominated National Government set up the London Passenger Transport Board. The *Industrial Charter* of 1947 committed the Conservative Party to a mixed economy. Returned to office in 1951, the Conservative Party accepted all the nationalisation measures, except for iron and steel which it denationalised in 1953, and road haulage which it denationalised in 1954.

Meanwhile, the Labour Party became less ambitious about nationalisation. The manifesto for the 1955 General Election promised merely to renationalise iron and steel and road haulage, and take over sections of chemicals and machine tools. In 1959, apart from retaining the commitment to 'restore steel to full public ownership' and 'restore public ownership in road haulage', the manifesto said only that 'if — after full and careful enquiry — other industries are found to be failing the nation, we shall not hesitate to use whatever remedies, including further public ownership, are shown to be most effective' (*The future Labour offers You*, The Labour Party, 1959). After the Labour Party's third successive election defeat in 1959, the party leader, Hugh Gaitskell, tried to get the party to rewrite Clause IV of the party constitution. He argued that the clause's open–ended commitment to public ownership laid the party open to damaging charges that it wished to nationalise everything. The party refused to agree. However, apart from the renationalisation of iron and steel, the 1964–70 Labour Government did little.

In opposition between 1966 and 1970, the Conservative Party became more sympathetic to the free economy. The Heath Government, 1970–74, started out in 1970 with such policies. In a House of Commons debate on 4 November 1970 John Davies, the Secretary of State for Trade and Industry, said that the country's essential need was 'to gear its policies to the great majority of people, who are not lame ducks, who do not need a hand, who are quite capable of looking after their own interests and only demand to be allowed to do so'. However, by 1972 the government U-turned, giving a hand to 'lame ducks' Rolls-Royce and the Upper Clyde Shipyard by taking them into public ownership. The Industry Act, 1972, empowered the government to intervene on a large scale in firms. In 1974 the Conservative Party's *Campaign Guide* accepted the status quo on the mixed economy and dismissed the prospect of denationalisation: 'Conservatives much prefer private enterprise to run a high proportion of the economy but it is simply not feasible to sell off all the nationalised industries regardless of price or consequences. In many instances, the industries are natural monopolies and must remain subject to public control'.

After its 1970 election defeat the Labour Party moved to the left. *Labour's Programme* 1973 proposed the creation of a National Enterprise Board (NEB) to take a controlling interest in twenty-five of the largest manufacturers. The Labour Government of 1974–9 was more cautious. It took into public ownership the aerospace and shipbuilding industries, both of which were already receiving substantial state aid. In 1975 it also established the NEB, with powers to make voluntary planning agreements with firms and extend public ownership. However, the NEB did little beyond rescuing financially troubled firms, buying a share of the ailing Chrysler car company and 95 per cent of Leyland car company.

Active Government
Keynes obviously provided an important justification for active government in economic management. In the early 1960s governments adopted economic planning, established targets for economic growth, consulted with the two sides

of industry, and even, in 1965, drew up a National Plan. The first serious post–war attempt to break with interventionist government was Heath's administration in 1970. It announced tax cuts and cut back the rate of increase in public spending. However, by 1973 the spending cuts were reversed.

Welfare

The *Beveridge Report* of 1942 put forward a Plan for Social Security which included as it main method compulsory social insurance, with national assistance and voluntary insurance as subsidiary methods. It assumed allowances for dependent children as part of its background, also the establishment of comprehensive health and rehabilitation services and maintenance of employment. In 1946 family allowances were made available from general taxation, and a National Insurance Act established an extended system of national insurance providing flat-rate payments by way of unemployment benefit, sickness benefit, maternity benefit, retirement pension, widows' benefits, guardians' allowance and death grant. The National Assistance Act in 1948 covered those who did not have a complete contributions record. In 1948 the National Health Service was established to provide free medical services for all at the point of entry.

The main features of the welfare state were largely accepted by Conservative governments in the 1950s. However, in the 1960s some Conservatives became doubtful about the principle of universality, looking more favourably on the idea of selectivity as a means both of reducing the rising costs of welfare and of concentrating help on those most in need.

Conciliation of the Trade Unions

An implicit 'policy consensus' on union–government relations had three main features (Kavanagh and Morris, 1989).

1 The need for a *national wages policy*. Both Keynes and Beveridge had been worried about the potential inflationary effects of free collective bargaining in a situation of near full employment. The 1944 White Paper stated: 'if ... we are to operate with success a policy for maintaining a high and stable level of employment, it will be essential that employers and workers should exercise moderation in wage matters' (para 49, p. 18). The Labour Government operated a voluntary incomes policy with some success from 1948 until 1950. Succeeding Conservative governments relied on exhortation, warnings, and occasionally restraint in the public sector as an example to the workforce as a whole. The combination of steadily improving living standards during the 1950s and a deliberate policy of conciliation of the trade unions by the Ministry of Labour helped to avoid any major confrontation between government and the unions. In 1961, however, the Conservative Government declared a six–month freeze on pay rises, to be enforced by government decision in the public sector but left to employers to apply in the private

sector. Following this, the government established the National Incomes Commission (NIC), to which contentious pay agreements were referred for public comment. The trade unions would have nothing to do with the NIC and it was soon wound up.

Restraint on incomes soon emerged at the forefront of the policy of the 1964–70 Labour Government. In 1965 the government established a National Board for Prices and Incomes (NBPI), to which proposed wage increases were to be referred and which had the power to impose a three–month standstill. The Labour Party won the 1966 General Election committed to a voluntary prices and incomes policy, but this was followed by a statutory one which lasted until 1969 with the 1970 General Election in sight.

The Conservative Government elected in 1970 was committed to less government intervention and therefore to no statutory control of prices and incomes. It abolished the NBPI. However, in 1972 the government introduced a wage freeze followed by rigid limits on pay rises, establishing the Pay Board and Price Commission. There was confrontation with the NUM over implementation of stage 3 of the policy in the winter of 1973/4. Heath called a general election in February 1974 which the Conservative Party lost.

Meanwhile, relations between the trade unions and the Labour Party had substantially improved. The result was the development of what came to be called the Social Contract, under which there was a voluntary agreement over prices and incomes policy. Initially, the trade unions and the Labour Government, 1974–9, entered into a loose agreement on wages policy, but subsequently agreement was reached on three stages between 1975 and 1978 which proved successful in restricting wage levels.

2 The *involvement of trade unions* in management of the economy. Fascination with active government contributed to a desire to involve the TUC and the CBI in economic management. The institutional consequence of this desire for cooperation in economic management was the creation by Macmillan's Government in 1962 of the National Economic Development Council (NEDC). Its role was, as the Conservative Party manifesto in 1964 said, to give 'reality to the democratic concept of planning by partnership'.

The TUC–Labour Party Liaison Committee formed in 1972 was the structural manifestation of the significantly changed relationship between the Labour Party and the TUC. It was composed of six representatives each from the General Council of the TUC, the National Executive Committee of the Labour Party and the Parliamentary Labour Party. The Committee was crucially involved in the development of the Social Contract.

3 A need for *measures of legal restraint*. After the Labour Government came into office in 1964 it appointed in 1965 a Royal Commission under Lord Donovan to carry out a 'high level and searching inquiry into the role of both the trade unions' and the employers' organisations in a modern society'. When the Donovan Report finally appeared in 1968 it concluded that legislation was of

limited utility in the field of industrial relations. Nevertheless, the government proposed, in the White Paper, *In Place of Strife*, (1969), new measures for government intervention in the field of industrial relations, including penal sanctions against offending trade unions and trade unionists. The proposals met with major opposition among trade unions, the Labour Party, Labour MPs and sections of the Cabinet led by Callaghan. After a protracted struggle, the government was forced to withdraw its proposals and accept trade union assurances that they would deal with some of the problems voluntarily.

Meanwhile, the Conservative Party under the leadership of Heath published a policy document, *Fair Deal at Work*, in 1968 which suggested that trade unions should operate in a legal framework and be held legally responsible for the actions of members. In 1970, for the first time since the war, industrial relations figured as a prominent issue in a general election. The Conservative Party won the election with a commitment to introduce a Bill to 'put unions on a legal footing', a major plank of their election manifesto. The 1971 Industrial Relations Act was passed after little prior consultation with the TUC. It extended the traditional remedies and procedures of the civil law to the problems of industrial relations. Aggrieved parties would have the right to apply to the courts for remedies, the institutional heart of the legislation laying in the National Industrial Relations Court (NIRC). The General Council of the TUC advised affiliated unions not to register under the Act and the few that did so were subsequently expelled. It also advised unions not to cooperate with the NIRC and to attend its proceedings only when an action was brought against them. Overall, the action of the trade unions, together with a marked reluctance on the part of large companies and employers' organisations to use its provisions for fear of damaging relations with employees, turned the act, or at least most of its provisions, into a virtual dead letter. Indeed, in the run up to the February 1974 General Election, in a widely reported 'off the record' speech, Campbell Adamson, the Director General of the CBI, spoke in favour of a repeal of the Act, which he saw as almost inoperable and damaging to industrial relations. The Labour Government after the February 1974 general Election repealed the 1971 Industrial Relations Act. In October 1974 the Conservative Party manifesto made only passing reference to it.

BREAKDOWN OF THE POST–WAR CONSENSUS

There had long been minorities in the major parties who dissented from the policies of the post–war consensus. In the face of a gathering economic recession, which followed the sharp increase in Arab oil prices in 1973–4, a slow-down of economic growth, and the clear repudiation of each party in government in the February 1974 and 1979 elections, these critics found greater support.

Full Employment

Inflation reached an annual rate of 26 per cent in July 1975. The Labour Government changed course. In March 1975 Dennis Healey's budget 'abandoned the full–employment goal' (Kavanagh, 1997). With unemployment exceeding one million, the budget would have been expected to reduce taxes and/or increase public spending. Instead, Healey did the opposite, choosing to reduce, instead of increase, the budget deficit. In his first speech to the party conference as prime minister in 1976 Callaghan proclaimed the new thinking: 'We used to think that you could just spend your way out of recession and increase employment only by cutting taxes and boosting government expenditure.... it only worked by injecting bigger doses of inflation into the economy followed by a higher level of unemployment at the next step'. He concluded that the option of spending yourself out of a recession 'no longer exists'.

The switch in policy was confirmed by the 1976 International Monetary Fund (IMF) rescue package for sterling. After it the government was forced to reduce the public sector borrowing requirement (PSBR), cash limit much central and local government spending, and set targets for controlling the money supply. Unemployment doubled over the lifetime of the 1974–9 Labour Government to 1.2 million or 6.2 per cent.

By the mid-seventies it was possible to distinguish three policies among economists for achieving high employment and stable prices. The neo–Keynesians of the National Institute of Economic Research wanted to curb inflation with an incomes policy while still pursuing Keynesian policies of economic growth. A second group, the Cambridge School, identified with the Department of Applied Economics at Cambridge University, argued that since Britain's manufacturing was uncompetitive, the home market would have to be protected by import controls and, if necessary, an incomes police, in order to suppress inflationary tendencies when demand was boosted. The group's call for import controls achieved some influence in the left wing of the Labour Party and was incorporated in its alternative socialist strategy. Finally, there was a growing school of monetarists who argued that the key to reducing inflation was to control the money supply. Inspired by Friedman and Hayek, they claimed that inflation was always a monetary problem and that incomes policy was thus irrelevant. If wage bargainers pushed for inflationary wage increases (that is, at a level above that of output), this would result in an increase in unit costs, a decline in competitiveness, a loss of markets, and the destruction of jobs. People educated in these 'facts' of economic life would then change their behaviour and bargain 'responsibly'.

Trade Unions

In the winter of 1978–9, Callaghan's Labour Government failed to reach agreement with the TUC over stage 4 of the voluntary incomes policy. The government unilaterally declared a 5 per cent voluntary limit which was widely broken. There were damaging strikes, often unofficial and largely in the public sector. In December 1978 the Ford Motor Company eventually settled a strike at the cost of a 15 per cent wage rise and a similar figure settled a strike of BBC technicians. In the New Year there was an outburst of strikes and militant picketing by lorry drivers, ambulance drivers, oil–tanker drivers, and local government workers which resulted in the closure of schools, disruption of hospitals, and in one well-publicised case a refusal to bury the dead. The 'Winter of Discontent' discredited cooperation with the trade unions.

Welfare

The agreement about the role, and satisfaction with the performance, of the welfare state gradually weakened. There were differences among Conservative critics, but all professed concern about the mounting costs of the universal provision involved in the Beveridge proposals which were not designed to cope with large numbers of unemployed and elderly, together with the growing number of family breakdowns. The system failed to concentrate resources on the most needy. They therefore favoured more selectivity in the distribution of welfare resources and encouraging people to take out private insurance to relieve the burden on the state.

On the Left academic research by Titmuss, Townsend and Abel Smith showed that the welfare state had not succeeded in eliminating poverty.

A number of Marxist and neo–Marxist writers claimed that the slowdown of economic growth was producing a new 'contradiction' in advanced capitalist societies. High levels of welfare spending were necessary to gain popular support but, increasingly, this was achieved at the cost of squeezing the profits of industry. Hence the 'contradiction', of fiscal crisis, of the capitalist state, arising from the conflicting needs to maintain public support and provide for capital accumulation (O'Connor).

A Mixed Economy

The Conservative Party manifesto for the 1979 General Election said the party would offer 'to sell back to private ownership the recently nationalised aerospace and shipbuilding concerns'. It aimed 'to sell shares in the National Freight Corporation'. It would 'restrict the powers of the National Enterprise Board solely to the administration of the Government's temporary shareholdings, to be sold off as circumstances permit'. It wanted 'to see those industries that remain nationalised running more successfully' and would 'therefore interfere less with their management and set them a clearer financial discipline in which to work' (*The Conservative manifesto*, 1979). Privatisation emerged as economic concerns over public spending and continued losses in some nationalised industries led Conservative ministers to seek a new approach.

Active Government

Answers to the question of why Britain was becoming harder to govern in the 1970s highlighted the problem of overload. There should be more concern with 'how the number of tasks that government has come to be expected to perform can be reduced' (King, 1976). The Conservative Party manifesto in 1979 agreed: 'Attempting to do too much, politicians have failed to do those things which *should* be done. This has damaged the country and the authority of government. We must concentrate on what should be the priorities for *any* government' (*The Conservative manifesto*, 1979).

THATCHERISM

As a set of policies Thatcherism rested on four main principles (Kavanagh, 1997).

1 The determination to reduce the rate of growth in money supply so that inflation would be squeezed out of the system. This involved the abandonment of formal incomes policies and 'deals' between government, employers, and trade unions as part of an attack on inflation. If the two sides of industry settled for a rate of increase in wages higher than the growth in productivity, they ran the risk of losing markets and pricing themselves out of jobs.

2 The reduction in the public sector and encouragement of a free-market-orientated economy. This involved setting tight financial targets for the nationalised industries and, eventually, the privatisation of state-owned industries and services, removing 'stifling' regulations on business, and encouraging the sale of council houses. The government would not bail out or subsidise loss–making industries indefinitely. Lower public spending would facilitate tax cuts and these in turn would encourage economic growth and the creation of new firms.

3 The government to free the labour market and encourage responsible trade union practices through reforms (see Simpson, 1999, p. 19–21). Control of the money supply had to work in tandem with the creation of a more effective free–market economy.

4 The restoration of the authority of government. This involved, on the one hand, both strengthening the nation's military defence and forces of law and order and, on the other, resisting damaging claims of pressure groups. There would be significant increases in resources for the armed forces and police. Pressure groups would be curbed by limiting the responsibilities of government, for example in maintaining full employment, and by the firm control of public spending.

In all, the four policies married the values of a free economy and a strong state (see page 43). The ideas, particularly those about relations between individuals and the state, amounted to a forceful assault on the post–war consensus.

The Labour Party's reaction to Thatcherism

The Labour Party had to come to terms with the scale of its defeat in the 1979 General Election and what it signified about its record in government. Initially, the party led by Michael Foot moved to the left in its support for further measures of public ownership, and its opposition to membership of the European Economic Community and nuclear weapons.

This led to the emergence of the Social Democratic Party in 1981. During 1979–80 two forces combined to assist its creation. The first factor was the growing disillusion of a number of substantial figures in the Labour Party with what was happening to the party. In the end it was the 'Gang of Three', Shirley Williams (out of Parliament), Bill Rodgers, and David Owen who opened the path to a breakaway party. These were all members of the previous Labour Government and could reasonably have expected to hold office in a future one. The second factor was the availability of Roy Jenkins, whose term of office as President of the European Commission was due to end in January 1981; he was looking for a means of re–entry to British politics. Jenkins had left a post in the Labour Cabinet in 1976 to take up the Presidency, but was now disenchanted with what was happening to the party. In March 1981 the new Social Democratic Party (SDP) was formally launched, supported now by fourteen Labour MPs and one Conservative MP. Within twelve months the number of MPs had grown to twenty-nine, thanks to further defections from the Labour Party and two by–election successes.

The Labour Party's manifesto for the 1983 General Election was its most radical, socialist programme in over fifty years. It said that the Labour Party would 'return to public ownership the public assets' hived off by the Conservative Government, 'with compensation of no more than that received when the assets were denationalised'. The Labour Party, 'committed to radical, socialist policies for reviving the British economy', was bound to find continued membership of the EEC 'a most serious obstacle to the fulfilment of those policies'. Thus, 'British withdrawal from the Community' was the right policy for Britain 'to be completed well within the lifetime of the parliament'. That was the Labour Party's commitment. Another commitment was a 'non–nuclear defence policy' for Britain carried through 'in the lifetime of the next parliament' (*The New Hope for Britain*, 1983). One shadow minister termed Labour's 1983 manifesto 'the longest suicide note in history'. In terms of votes cast per candidate, the result of the 1983 General Election was the Labour Party's worst since its creation in 1900, and it was only just ahead of the SDP/Liberal Alliance in its share of the vote. This ended the first phase of the Labour Party's reaction to Thatcherism.

By the time of the 1987 General Election changes had been made to Labour Party policies under the leadership of Neil Kinnock. Pledges to extend 'social ownership' were confined to British Telecom and British Gas. The Labour Party's aim was 'to work constructively with out EEC partners to promote economic expansion and combat unemployment', though it would 'stand up for British interests within the European Community' and 'like other member countries, reject EEC interference' with its policy for recovery and renewal. After consultation, the Labour Party would inform the Americans that it wished them 'to remove their cruise missiles and other nuclear weapons from Britain'. (*Britain will win*, 1987).

Following Thatcher's third successive election victory in 1987, the Labour Party instituted a major examination of its policies. The two-year policy review culminated in the publication in 1989 of a 70,000 word document, *Meet the Challenge Make the Change*. In 1990 a revised, slimmer 20,000 word document, *Looking to the Future*, provided some significant policy refinements, particularly in the field of the economy. The review provided a clear indication that the Labour Party now accepted an important role for the market. There was no shopping list of industries and services to be nationalised and, particularly in the initial document, the review was remarkably cautious even about taking the public utilities back into public ownership. On Europe, the review called for increased co-operation with the other member-states of the EEC. It abandoned unilateral nuclear disarmament in favour of bilateral and multilateral initiatives. However, the difference between the two major parties still remained in that the Labour Party envisaged 'major state intervention and regulation in all areas of the economy as a key to the promotion of the twin aims of social justice and economic efficiency' (Garner, 1990).

Major's Impact
Continuity between Thatcherism and Major stands out:

- Major and Thatcher shared the vision of a low tax economy.
- Privatisation was maintained. The Major Government privatised two of the most difficult candidates, British Rail and British Coal, and sold off the nuclear industry.
- The NEDC was abolished in 1992, and wages councils were abolished. However, the actions were largely symbolic, because both bodies had been weakened in the preceding years.
- The creation of executive agencies in the civil service was continued.
- Major's main impact was on the public services, but even here there was continuity. Under the third Thatcher Government, loans for students in higher education were introduced, the health service reforms had just started and the Housing Act allowed council house tenants to opt for private landlords. Major's search for mechanisms other than privatisation to give people more opportunity and choice resulted in the Citizen's Charter in 1991. Thatcher's notion of empowerment allowed little scope for providing means of redress of grievances beyond facilitating opt-outs of schools and council tenants from local authorities.

- Having rejected large-scale privatisation of health and education, the Major Government sought to import the best of private sector management practice as a means of improving the performance of these services. This included performance related pay, audit, competition and more information about standards. League tables reported each school's performances on the national curriculum tests, public examinations, and truancy. The government also tried to mobilise consumers to expect and demand a high level of service. They should be able to complain, insist on value for money, and ultimately be reimbursed or compensated for poor service. In health, the devices were internal markets, hospital trusts, and fund–holding doctors; in schools, a national curriculum, testing, and the right for schools to control their own budgets. These were all set in train by 1960, but the Major Government implemented them energetically.

- The Charter has been Major's initiative. It is a philosophy of administration as well as an attempt to change the culture of the public service. Consumers are provided with more information about their rights and the performance of services. Deliverers of services are set targets for improved performance, faced with more competition, independent inspection and better complaints procedures for consumers. There are sharper divisions now between consumers of the services, on the one hand, and producers and providers, on the other. At the heart of the Charter is the notion of the citizen as an individual consumer of public services and of a new relationship between the client and the provider of the service. The election and accountability of government are missing from this equation, with services being contracted out to such bodies as grant-maintained schools and hospital trusts. (Kavanagh, 1997).

NEW LABOUR

After the Labour Party's unexpected fourth successive defeat in 1992, party leaders were convinced that it was their tax-and-spend proposals which had prevented the party from winning. There were determined, particularly after Blair became leader following the death of Kinnock's successor, John Smith, in 1994, to avoid any policy commitments which the Conservative Party could cost and translate into tax increases.

The Shadow Chancellor, Gordon Brown, ruled out any increase in borrowing in a speech on 18 May 1995. He offered more independence to the Bank of England and promised to bear down on inflation. In January 1997, he pledged not to increase the top rate or the standard rate of income tax and promised to freeze public spending totals for the next two years. The Labour Party made few explicit spending pledges, being determined to deny the Conservative Party opportunities to translate these into taxes. Any new outlays were to be funded by switching spending from elsewhere. For example, if the assisted places scheme were ended it would release money to fund lower class sizes in primary schools; if taxes were earmarked it would be possible to use a windfall tax on the profits of the privatised utilities to finance an attack on youth employment. Crucial to any plans to control public spending was how to curb the rising costs of social security. The Labour Party floated ideas about workfare, and its welfare-to-work scheme made receipt of benefits conditional on seeking work or receiving training. The 1992 election promises to upgrade child benefit and pensions, and to link future pension increases to movements in prices or earnings (whichever was the higher) were abandoned.

The Labour Party manifesto for the 1997 General Election, *New Labour Because Britain Deserves Better*, focused on the party's five-year 'contract with the people':

1 Education will be our number one priority, and we will increase the share of national income spent on education as we decrease it on the bills of economic and social failure.
2 There will be no increase in the basic or top rates of income tax.
3 We will provide stable economic growth with low inflation, and promote dynamic and competitive business and industry at home and abroad.
4 We will get 250,000 young unemployed off benefit and into work.
5 We will rebuild the NHS, reducing spending on administration and increasing spending on patient care.
6 We will be tough on crime and tough on the causes of crime, and halve the time it takes persistent juvenile offenders to come to court.
7 We will help build strong families and strong communities, and lay the foundations of a modern welfare state in pensions and community care.
8 We will safeguard our environment, and develop an integrated transport policy to fight congestion and pollution.
9 We will clean up politics, decentralise political power throughout the United Kingdom and put the funding of political parties on a proper and accountable basis.
10 We will give Britain the leadership in Europe which Britain and Europe need.

There were five election pledges:

1 cut class sizes to 30 or under for 5, 6 and 7 year–olds by using money from the assisted places scheme;
2 fast–track punishment for persistent young offenders by halving the time from arrest to sentencing;
3 cut NHS waiting lists by treating an extra 100,000 patients as a first step by releasing £100 million saved from NHS red tape;
4 get 250,000 under–25 year–olds off benefit and into work by using money from a windfall levy on the privatised utilities:
5 no rise in income tax rates, cut VAT on heating to 5 per cent and inflation and interest rates as low as possible.

A NEW CONSENSUS

Many policy goals and views are broadly shared across the political spectrum, although the policies differ from those of the post–war consensus. The main features of the new consensus are:

- A narrowing of choice in macro-economic policy. The UK's membership of the ERM between October 1989 and September 1992 largely determined decisions on public spending, interest rates and borrowing. Even out of the ERM, however, economic policies have to take account of the likely reactions of financial markets. In a global economy national governments can pay a heavy price pursuing policies regarded as 'imprudent'. On the eve of the General Election of 1997, the Labour Party decided to accept the Conservative tax and public spending totals for the following two years. Within a few days of taking office the Blair Government gave the Bank of England control over the setting of interest rates.
- A greater reliance on markets for wealth creation and, to a lesser extent, allocation of welfare. The leaderships in both parties still remain tentative in pushing the idea of markets further on welfare because of perceived public resistance, and the Labour Party prefers more management of markets. However, all the major parties now clearly accept the market as more effective in promoting greater choice. Private ownership of the utilities is now common ground, although there are differences about the rigour of their regulation.
- A need for public services to be more responsive to consumers. There is a shared concern with promoting the rights of consumers of services, and establishing more equal relations between consumers and producers. The new outlook is consistent with the Labour Party's weakening of its link with the trade unions, particularly public–sector trade unions.
- An emphasis on cost–containment and value for money in the public sector. The strategies of new public management are here to stay, given the voters' demand for better public services, alongside a resistance to pay more income tax and constraints on increased public spending.
- A rethinking of the range of services and benefits which the state provides, for example through more selectivity and opting out, and of new ways to finance them, for example through increased charges and private provision.
- A concern at how some of the social and economic policies of the 1980s have weakened the sense of community.
- A turning–away from top–down provision in universal services; greater flexibility and competition, as in schools and higher education, is the order of the day. In some ways, this is less a European than a North American model of government (partly because of federalism, partly because of a more modest state role as provider of welfare, and partly because of the lower social and political status of the federal bureaucracy).

(Kavanagh, 1997).

The new agenda has grown out of the Thatcherite policies of the 1980s particularly in respect of the following:

Economic liberalism
This includes the acceptance of privatisation, a low inflation target, curbing government borrowing, insisting on tough convergence conditions for a single European currency, and freeing the Bank of England to control interest rates.

Flexible markets
The industrial relations legislation, 1980–93, remains in place. A minimum wage was introduced at a relatively low level. Although the Social Charter was accepted, Blair has presented in the European Union the case for the Anglo–Saxon model of flexible labour market against the 'social market' model of his European Socialist colleagues.

Social conservatism
This has been reflected in proposals that offenders make reparations for damage done to property and persons, that incompetent teachers be rooted out, tough criteria be imposed for receiving long–term sickness and unemployment benefits, and that measures be taken to reduce the social security budget.

Paradoxically, the General Election of 1997 'produced the biggest electoral change in votes and seats in the twentieth century but was accompanied by such a modest shift about the role of government and the balance between public and private sector and between tax and spending' (Kavanagh, 1997).

Hague's 'Common Sense Revolution'
In October 1999 Hague unveiled a radical programme promising tax cuts and greater private sector provision in education, health and welfare provision. A policy document, *The Common Sense Revolution*, contained five guarantees.

1 The Parents' Guarantee would 'give parents the power to change school management that fails to deliver adequate standards' (Conservative Party, 1999b). Where inspection confirmed that the school was not delivering an acceptable quality of education, the Local Education Authority would be required to put the management of the school out to tender.
2 The Patient's Guarantee would 'give every NHS patient a guaranteed waiting time based on their need for treatment'. If the NHS's own facilities could not do the job, the NHS would get private sector contractors to do it.
3 The Tax Guarantee that 'taxes will fall as a share of the nation's income over the term of the next Parliament under a Conservative Government'.
4 The Can Work, Must Work Guarantee would ensure that 'benefit claimants who can work but won't work, will lose their unemployment benefit'. Local job centres would be contracted out to private sector firms which would be paid by their success in getting people into jobs. The Employment Service would be given new powers to 'flush out scroungers and shirkers'.

5 The Sterling Guarantee that the Conservative Party would 'oppose entry into the Single Currency at the next election as part of our manifesto for the next Westminster Parliament'.

CHANGING PARTY IMAGES

SPIN DOCTORS AND MEDIA ADVISERS

Initially, 'spin' was a term reserved for the practice of putting the best possible gloss on an event breaking in the news. Typically, after a presidential debate in the USA spokespersons from both sides 'would rush — literally, run — to the awaiting media corps to give their line on the debate' (Gould, 1998). This was called 'spinning', putting your perspective on what happened. In 1996 Gould was in the media area after a presidential debate. 'It had a huge sign over its saying SPIN CITY. The moment the debate started it was as though the floodgates opened.... The place was in complete turmoil — crushed, heaving, shouting, maniacal. At points just yards apart campaign representatives were spinning, putting their views of the debate'. So-called spin doctors, media advisers 'who will coax the media into carrying favourable interpretation of events', are 'a part of a modern communications system' in political parties. (Butler and Kavanagh, 1997).

Media advisers are responsible for media relations for a political party. David Hill, former chief media adviser for the Labour Party, describes how he works:

> *"The first rule is you have to understand and know the people you are dealing with.... You've got to be robust, you've got to understand your journalists, you've got to never lie to them, and you have got to recognise what they want. You have got to have speed, because if you don't get your strike in first, or if you don't follow something up quickly, then you get left behind. You must provide words, because they always need words. What you have got to do to be ... someone who can really do the business on behalf of the party ... is to be someone who the media can go to and say: 'Although I have got a story, if I've spoken to you I know the status of an issue. I know where it is taking me, I know whether it is going to take off or not.' Then you will have created a relationship with the journalists which is pivotal." However, critics complain of 'a mixture of bullying and flattery applied to journalists'.*
>
> *(Gould, 1998).*

> *However, critics complain of 'a mixture of bullying and flattery applied to journalists'.*
>
> *(Butler and Kavanagh, 1997).*

New Labour
According to Gould, it was Alastair Campbell, Blair's Press Secretary, who turned the phrase '*New Labour*' into an entirely new identity for the Labour Party. "We wanted a slogan for conference.... Alastair was working on some alternatives. We were in a meeting and Alastair, as is his way, scribbled down

several lines, which he showed to me. One was: 'New Labour, New Britain'." (Gould, 1998). The slogan was used at the party conference in 1994. Putting New Labour in massive letters in front of hundreds of delegates was 'effectively renaming the party…. This was the moment New Labour became a reality'.

Rebranding the Conservative Party

Danny Finklestein, Director of the Conservative Party Research Department, argued that the result of the 1997 general election was 'a vote against Conservatives, not Conservatism', because the electorate saws the Conservatives as 'arrogant, smug, sleazy, weak, incompetent and divided'. ('Why did so many voters desert us for New Labour? *The Independent*, 13 October 1998). In other words, the party needed to rebrand its image. Addressing a meeting at Conservative Central Office on 23 July 1997, soon after his selection as leader following the 'disaster' of the election defeat on May 1, Hague said that if the Conservatives were to win acceptance and popular support once again, they had to show that they understood why the voters rejected them. 'Let us show the British people that we have learnt from our experience', he added (Conservative Party, 1997).

Project Hague

PROJECT HAGUE

Key Themes

Strong relationships (with family, friends)
Activities (fit/active person, team player, life beyond politics)
Yorkshire (strong roots, solidity, committed to constituency)
Theme ❏ Photo ❏ Message ❏ Timing ❏ ❏ 2 ❏ Abseiling in constituency ❏ Not an action shot – chance to reinforce Yorkshire message as well ❏ 26 June ❏ ❏ 3 ❏ Return to Wath school – jacket off, talking to pupils ❏ Went to comprehensive! Strong ties in Yorkshire ❏ 2 July ❏ ❏ 1/3 ❏ Yorkshire Show – with Marjorie and Peter (showing Texel sheep) ❏ Family roots in Yorkshire ❏ July 13 ❏ ❏ 1/3 ❏ Star Wars Premier – arrival shot with Ffion and nieces ❏ Family outing, close to nieces, tactile, happy shot ❏ 14 July ❏ ❏ 2/1 ❏ Walking in constituency with friends. Setting off on 3 Peaks Walk with friends (and army?). Regular summer activity, doing a punishing course in faster time each year ❏ Late July/early August? ❏ ❏ 1 ❏ Holiday shot with Ffion – evening walk on beach? Relaxing, quality time with wife ❏ August – probably best done abroad ❏ ❏ 2/1 ❏ Sailing – in USA, informal shot on board? Not action shot ❏ Teaching Ffion (or godson) to sail on holiday ❏ Late August ❏ ❏ 2 ❏ Judo with Army ❏ No shots of actual fight, shots with army fighters (in kit?) – in serious training for next belt. Blue belt to be attempted before Conference ❏ Early September ❏ ❏ 1 ❏ Pre-Conference shot with Ffion ❏ Relaxed and confident before Conference, another opportunity to do a casual photo ❏ 2/3 October ❏ ❏ 3/1 ❏ Muker – Doreen and chocolate cake ❏ Pre-conference walk in Dales, country pub, colourful locals etc ❏ W/e before conference ❏ ❏ 1 ❏ Conference – shot with all three sisters, (casual, in bar?) ❏ Family supporting WH, making big effort to be at conference – Veronica will have come from the USA ❏ October 4–8 ❏ ❏ 1 ❏ Conference – family dinner, informal, fun ❏ Relaxed, large family, as above October 4–8.
Ideas to be developed:
Illustration for Relative Values, with Marjorie – or more casual shot in Yorkshire.
Visiting troops in Kosoo – Brigadier Pearson, Commander of Catterick Garrison will shortly depart for Kosovo. He knows WH and would be happy to host a visit. WH to take messages over from families in Catterick Garrison?
Opportunity for another casual dress shot.

Source: *The Independent*, 13 August 1999.

PROJECT HAGUE: WILLIAM HAGUE'S ATTEMPTS TO USE PUBLICITY TO HIS ADVANTAGE

There were attempts to change the party leader's own image. Wearing a baseball cap emblazoned with his surname during a watershoot ride failed to change his image from a 'school swot' and a political 'trainspotter'. So did being pictured alongside his wife, Ffion, at the Notting Hill carnival in west London in shirt sleeves without a tie, sipping an exotic cocktail from a coconut. Early in the summer of 1999 a memo, known as Project Hague, was drawn up by senior party strategists to improve his image. Leaked to the *Daily Telegraph*, its key themes were:

'Strong relationships (with family, friends)

Activities (fit/active person, team player, life beyond politics)

Yorkshire (strong roots, solidity, committed to constituency)'

Ideas to improve his image included:

'Family outing, close to nieces, tactile, happy shot…. Walking in constituency with friends'

'Absailing in constituency…. Setting off on Peaks Walk with friends (and army?).

Regular summer activity, doing a punishing course in faster time each year…. Holiday shot with Ffion — evening walk on beach? Relaxing, quality time with wife'

'Return to Wath school… Strong ties in Yorkshire…. Yorkshire Show…. Family roots in Yorkshire'.

CONSULTING WIDER OPINION

Labour Listens
Running parallel with the Labour Party's policy review, 1987–9, was a *Labour Listens* campaign. By organising events throughout the country the Labour Party hoped to identify the greatest concerns of voters which could then be fed into the policy review process.

Listening to Britain
After the disastrous election defeat in 1997, Hague said that Conservatives must 'stop lecturing to people and start listening to them' (Conservative Party, 1997). A year later he launched the *Listening to Britain* campaign. *Listening to Britain* was a copy of the Republicans' 'Listening to America' which led to the 10 point manifesto 'Contract with America' which delivered the Republicans with victory in the 1984 Congressional elections soon after their defeat in the 1992 presidential election. In 1999, the Conservative Party claimed that *Listening to Britain* had been 'the most ambitious listening exercise ever undertaken by a British political party' (*Conservative Party*, 1999a). In its first year 40,000 people had attended over

1,400 meetings, 250,000 responses had been received to questionnaires, consultations and other requests for information. At every one of these meetings, a frontbencher or other senior party figure had been present to hear views and to take notes — 'to listen, not to lecture'. For the first time, Conservative Party policy–making was founded on 'wide-ranging consultation with the public'.

INVOLVEMENT OF NON-PARTY MEMBERS

PRIVATE POLLS AND FOCUS GROUPS

'No self-respecting party can now campaign without its own private polls' (Butler and Kavanagh, 1997). *Quantified opinion polls* with samples of over 1,000 are 'no longer snapshots of public opinion, they are incredibly perceptive measures of where public opinion is, long questionnaires with subtle and intelligent questions' (Gould, 1998). For the 1997 election and pre-election period the Labour Party had the voluntary assistance of the American pollster, Stanley Greenberg.

Focus groups are structured discussions with a small number of carefully selected voters. The eight or so members of a group will have been recruited by a research company according to a formal specification: who they voted for in a previous election, their age, their occupation. Gould nearly always conducted them 'in unassuming front rooms in Watford, or Edgware or Milton Keynes or Huddersfield, in a typical family room stacked with the normal knick-knacks and photos' (Gould, 1998). They have been increasingly used by the political parties, partly under the influence of American campaigning practice, and partly in reaction to the poor performance of the UK polls in 1992 (Butler and Kavanagh, 1997). From the time that Blair became leader of the Labour Party Gould 'did focus groups about once a week'. For the six and a half weeks of the 1997 General Election he 'conducted them six nights a week' (Gould, 1998). In February 1995 Gould attended focus groups conducted in Los Angeles by Greenberg for the President of the USA.

Greenberg has said of the use of modern polling techniques in political campaigning:

'It doesn't need defending. It is part of the democratisation of modern elections. Just as governments have changed, just as parties have changed, campaigns have changed. Democracy has changed. The institutions that used to be effective in mediating popular sentiment have atrophied, and have lost their ability to articulate. So the trade unions, for example, just don't have the kind of base that they used to have. If you want to know what working people think, you can't turn to these organisations which can effectively represent their members and so there is no choice but to go to people directly through these means'.

(Gould interview with Greenberg 2 July 1998, Gould, 1998).

SUMMARY

Consensus has been the norm in British politics since 1945. The Conservative Party adapted itself to the post–war political consensus which existed until its breakdown in the mid–970s. Thatcherism created a new consensus after 1979 which the Labour Party gradually accepted by the time of the 1987 general election onwards.

The phrase 'New Labour' was turned into an entirely new identity for the Labour Party under Tony Blair in 1994. After the disastrous election defeat for the Conservative Party in 1997, William Hague rebranded the party's image.

A *Labour Listens* campaign ran parallel with the Labour Party's policy review following Margaret Thatcher's third successive election victory in 1987. Hague launched the Conservative Party's *Listening to Britain* campaign after 1997.

Private polls and focus groups have been increasingly used by the political parties.

STUDY GUIDE

Revision hints

You should have some knowledge of the contemporary programmes being promoted by the parties.

Consider the rise of so-called spin doctors and media advisers in the parties to provide input on image and policy presentation; the use of private polls and focus groups in place of the views of the mass membership.

Exam hints

Answering structured stimulus questions
1   Study the extract below and answer **all** the questions which follow.

It is not easy for a party which has dominated government for much of the Twentieth Century to adapt readily to opposition. Party morale inevitably suffers. It is even harder when that party has enjoyed eighteen consecutive years in power but loses office in a massive defeat as the Conservatives did in the 1997 General Election. In addition opinion polls continue to show limited public awareness of key figures in the Shadow Cabinet.

The Conservatives are clearly in deep trouble. The Party has debts of £11 million; it is divided over important constitutional issues; and senior figures overshadow William Hague. Furthermore, Labour is now more popular than when it was elected. Even the Conservative Party's former supporter "The Sun" newspaper has dubbed it a "dead parrot".

Many party loyalists are pessimistic, fearing a long period in Opposition, and this situation could be made even worse if electoral reform produces Labour and Lib–Dem Coalitions.

Adopted from Politics, PAL, 1999

(a) Why, according to the extract, is the role of opposition 'not easy'?

(b) Using the extract, as well as your own knowledge, analyse the reasons why the Conservatives are described as being in 'deep trouble'.

(c) To what extent has William Hague modernised the Conservative party?

(AQA GCE Government and Politics, Advanced Subsidiary/Advanced Specimen Units and Mark Schemes, Unit Gov 2: Parties and Pressure Groups, Assessment and Qualifications Alliance 1999).

Question 1(c) covers chaning party images. Demonstrate knowledge and understanding of the revamping of the Conservative party image. Identify parallels and connections between the modernisation techniques and tactics used by the Conservative party since 1997 and those of other parties.

2   Discuss the campaigning techniques of UK political parties.

Demonstrate knowledge and understanding of the rise of so–called spin doctors and media advisers in the parties to provide input on image and policy presentation; the use of private polls and focus groups in place of the views of the mass membership. Identify parallels and connections between the campaigning techniques used by the UK parties and those of parties in the USA.

Practice Questions

1   To what extent has New Labour accepted the Thatcherite programme?
2   Is the Conservative Party's 'common sense revolution' a Thatcherite programme?

6

STRUCTURE AND ORGANISATION
OF THE MAJOR PARTIES

Introduction

THIS CHAPTER WILL look at party structure and organisation. It will examine the selection and deselection procedures for leaders and candidates. Finally, it will study the policy making procedures of the major parties.

Key Points
- Party structures.
- Selection and deselection procedures for leaders and candidates.
- Policy making procedures.

PARTY STRUCTURES

THE CONSERVATIVE PARTY

Prior to 1998, the Conservative Party structure consisted of three separate components: the Parliamentary party; the National Union of Conservative and Unionist Associations (the National Union), enfolding all voluntary Conservative activity outside Parliament; and Conservative Central Office (CCO), the headquarters of paid officials outside Parliament. The Conservative Party in Parliament had long preceded the party's extra–Parliamentary structure. Created in 1867 by Disraeli, the Conservative party leader, the National Union had been organised, in the words of one of its founds, the MP, H.C. Raikes, as a 'handmaid' to the party leadership (1873 *Conservative Annual Conference Report*). Such an organisation would help to minimise the danger inherent in the Conservative Party's 'leap in the dark' of that year. The Second Reform Act had roughly doubled the electorate and, of particular importance, the new electors were mainly members of the working and lower middle classes in the urban areas. It is not surprising therefore that the earliest efforts of the National Union were devoted to wooing the newly enfranchised urban voters. The formation of the CCO in 1870 followed logically from the organisation of the National Union three years earlier, both the direct consequence of the expansion of the electorate (McKenzie, 1964).

Each of these three separate organisations had different but overlapping responsibilities and all had their own separate hierarchy. Sometimes the three organisations pursued different strategies and competing priorities. The party structure sometimes made it very difficult for people to work together with a common team spirit. The result was that information and understanding was not as widely shared across the party as it should have been. Too much time was spent relating one part of the organisation to another. There was too much internal politics and not enough outward campaigning. Worst of all, the members in the constituencies often felt disconnected from the leadership and the headquarters. They spent time and money meeting each other, but with too little satisfaction that they had been properly engaged in the political progress of the party. There was a sense of frustration that the views of party members were too often ignored, and many people throughout the party did not feel part of a cohesive force. To replace the 'collection of cosy cliques and separate power bases', Hague said that 'the various hierarchies must be streamlined and brought together in a single structure'. A new governing body responsible for the oversight of the whole party's organisation would ensure that that single structure worked well in practice. (*Conservative Party*, 1997).

In 1998, the three pillars of the old party, parliamentary, voluntary and professional, were drawn together in a single structure. The new governing body, known as the **Board**, is the supreme decision-making body in matters of party organisation and management. It consists of:

- The Chairman of the party who is appointed by the leader of the party and who chairs the Board in the absence of the leader and acts as the leader's representative on it;
- Two Deputy Chairmen, one of whom is Chairman of the National Conservative Convention (also established in 1998, to 'provide a focus' for he views of party members and 'act as a link' between the party leader and party members) and who, in the absence of the Chairman of the Board and the leader, chairs the Board; the other is appointed by the leader;
- Four further members elected by the National Conservative Convention;
- The elected Chairman of the 1922 Committee (comprising all MP's);
- The Conservative leader in the House of Lords;

- The elected Deputy Chairman of the Scottish Conservative and Unionist Party;
- The elected co–ordinating Chairman for Wales;
- The elected Chairman of the Conservative Councillors' Association;
- The Treasurer of the party, who is appointed by the leader;
- One further member who may, from time to time, be nominated by the leader subject to endorsement by the Board;
- A senior member of the professional staff of the party, who is nominated to serve on the Board by the Chairman of the Board;
- The Board may make one further appointment to its number, subject to the approval of the leader.

The Board has power to do anything which in its opinion relates to the management and administration of the party. It oversees all activities within the party and in particular is responsible for:

- the development and implementation of the strategies for the party, for its campaigning, organisation, membership, and fund–raising at a national, European and local level;
- the review and approval of the party's budgets, the monitoring of financial performance and the production and publication of annual accounts;
- the appointment of senior star within the party;
- the administration of the national membership list (via the Committee on Membership);
- the maintenance of the Approval List of Candidates' (via the Committee on Candidates);
- the oversight of the management and administration of constituency associations, including the power to recognise federations or other groupings of constituency associations;
- the cancellation or refusal of membership, in its absolute discretion, of any party member or prospective party member;
- the replacement or removal from office of any officer of a constituency association or recognised organisation;
- the establishment of a new or replacement constituency association;
- the withdrawal or refusal of membership of a constituency association;
- the management of the National Conservative Convention;
- the organisation of party conferences (via the Committee on Conferences);
- ensuring that women are properly involved and represented in all aspects of the party's work and organisation including, if appropriate, the maintenance of an organisation to promote the interests of women within the party;
- ensuring that young people are properly involved and represented in all aspects of the party's work and organisation including the maintenance of a

youth organisation to recruit young people to the party and communicating with them;
- the grant to organisations of the status of a recognised organisation, and the withdrawal of such status;
- the co–ordination and implementation of a national strategy with respect to electoral boundary changes;
- the resolution of any disputes within the party, however arising, as it sees fit;
- the implementation of the decisions of the Ethics and Integrity Committee (see Appendix 2);
- the overseeing of the procedure for the election of the leader of the party in accordance with the provision of the constitution.

(*Constitution of the Conservative Party*, February 1998).

Table 6: *The composition of the Board of the Conservative Party*		
APPOINTED BY THE LEADER	PARLIAMENTARY PARTY	VOLUNTARY PARTY
Party Chairman	Chairman of the 1922 Committee	Chairman of the National Convention
A Deputy Chairman		President of the National Convention
A Treasurer		3 members elected from the National Convention
Leader in the House of Lords		An elected representative of the Party in Scotland
A senior member of the professional staff		The Welsh Co–ordinating
		Chairman of the Association of Conservative Councillors

SOURCE: *The Fresh Future*, Conservative Party, 1998.

The changed party structure is more 'streamlined'. It is representative of the whole party. Elected representatives from the party's membership are the largest single group on the Board (see Table 6). However, the main effect may be an erosion of the autonomy of constituency associations. For example:

- Every association is required to produce annual objectives and a plan of activity for the following year. This should be provided to the Board in an annual report together with information on, for example, income and accounts (*Fresh Future*, 1998). Some associations, like Aylesbury, have vast resources which the CCO with its own debts had been unable to plunder, but 'the new structure could end this anomaly' (Kelly, 1999b).
- If the membership of any constituency association falls below a minimum level determined by the Board, or in other exceptional circumstances, the

Board may designate such constituency association a 'supported association'. Where the Board so decides, the area management executive (which acts as a co–ordinating body between the Board and constituency associations), working with the association officers, may appoint a representative, run local recruitment campaigns, supervise the election of officers and assume responsibility for the funds and finances of the association. If the area management executive resolves that a supported association is failing to co-operate with any appointed representative or failing to make reasonable efforts to improve its performance, the area management executive may require the supported association to draw up an action plan. If, after 12 months, the area management executive is of the opinion that the association officers have failed to make reasonable efforts to achieve the targets set out in the action plan, the area management executive may report to the Board recommending that any association officer or officers shall be removed and that new elections are held (*Constitution of the Conservative Party*, February 1998, paragraphs 50–4, p. 11).

THE LABOUR PARTY

'The structure of the Labour Party is a natural product of the party's genesis' (Minkin). It was created in 1900 by an alliance of trade union and socialist organisations and subsequently the organisations retained their independence, affiliating annually to the party and obtaining representation at its annual conference as separate units. To administer the party an Executive Committee, later known as the National Executive Committee (NEC), was elected at each annual conference. Seats on this body were apportioned between the union and socialist sections. These confederal characteristics became a permanent feature of the party's structure.

The party was formed following a decision of the Trades Union Congress (TUC). It owed its survival to the affiliation of trade unions whose interest in an independent party of labour had been stimulated by a series of judicial decisions which threatened to undermine their industrial bargaining position. The combined strength of the unions within the party was far greater than that of the three socialist organisations, the Fabian Society, the Independent Labour Party (ILP) and the Social Democratic Federation (SDF). At the party conference where votes and delegates were apportioned by size, the trade unionists were in a large majority. Hence by origin and composition the party was a trade union party, and the formal dominance of the trade unions became a feature of its structure.

By 1998, the trade unions had only 50 per cent of the votes at the party conference. They have 12 of the 32 seats on the NEC. There is separate, direct representation of Constituency Labour Parties (CLPs), government, and Parliamentary Labour Party (PLP) including the European Parliamentary Labour Party (EPLP). With their own sections on the NEC, ministers, MPs and MEPs are ineligible to stand in other sections. Local government and the EPLP have representatives on the NEC. There is provision for a black/Asian representative on the NEC when membership of the Black Socialists Society reaches a threshold of 2,500 and at least one third of eligible organisations affiliate to the National Black Socialists Society conference. Quotas in all sections with more than one representative ensures a minimum of 12 women on the 32–member NEC (see Table 7).

Table 7: *NEC membership*			
SECTION	NUMBER OF REPRESENTATIVES	MINIMUM QUOTA OF WOMEN	METHOD OF ELECTION
Leader	1	–	Ex-officio
Deputy	1	–	Ex-officio
Treasurer	1	–	Annual conference
Trade unions	12	6	Trade unions at annual conference
Constituency Labour Parties	6	3	One member one vote
Socialist societies	1	–	Socialist societies at annual conference
Young Labour	1	–	Young Labour conference
Government	3	1	
Parliamentary Labour Party (including EPLP)	3	1	MPs and MEPs
European Parliamentary Labour Party (Leader)	1	–	Ex-officio
Local government	2	1	Association of Labour Councillors
(Black Socialists Society)	(1)	(–)	(National Black Socialists Society conference)
Total	**32**	**12**	

SOURCE: Partnership in Power, The Labour Party, 1997, p. 9.

The NEC 'reflects all parts of the party', the separate, direct representation of CLPs 'ensuring genuine grassroots representation' (*Partnership in power*, 1997, Labour Party). However, MPs and MEPs being ineligible to stand in other sections precludes 'difficult' MPs such as Dennis Skinner from claiming to be the 'real voice of the party' (Kelly, 1998b). Nevertheless, the left–wing Grassroots Alliance won four of the six places in the CLP section in 1998, three in 1999. Dennis Skinner, the outspoken left–wing MP, was elected to the NEC in the PLP and EPLP section in 1999.

THE LIBERAL DEMOCRAT PARTY

The party has a federal structure, comprising three 'state' parties, one each for Scotland, Wales and England.

- The Federal Party is responsible for the preparation of UK–wide policy, Parliamentary elections and fund–raising. England, Scotland and Wales separately are responsible for the operation of local parties, selection procedures for prospective parliamentary candidates, the arrangements for collecting and renewing party memberships and policy matters relating to their state — though they can request the Federal Party to look after the development of policy matters in particular fields.
- The Federal Conference of the party meets at least twice yearly.
- The Federal Conference elects the majority of the members of the three Federal Committees (Executive, Policy and Conference). Each of these committees also includes representatives of the Parliamentary party, councillors, Scottish and Welsh parties. Election procedures ensure that at least a third of all those directly elected must be women, and at least a third men.
- The Federal Executive is responsible for directing, co–ordinating and implementing the work of the Federal Party and is chaired by the President, who is elected for a two–year term by all members of the party. The Conference Committee is responsible for organising the two annual conferences, including selecting their agendas. The Policy Committee is responsible for initiating and developing policy proposals and, in conjunction with the Parliamentary party, for drawing up the party's general election and European election manifestos.

SELECTION AND DESELECTION PROCEDURES FOR LEADERS

THE LEADER OF THE PARTY

The Conservative Party
The new selection procedure (February 1998), which has yet to be implemented, takes place in two stages. The first stage will include only MPs, who will present

a choice of candidates to the whole party. The second stage will include party members who will vote to select the leader.

- The leader shall be drawn from MPs. The rules for deciding the procedure by which the 1922 Committee selects candidates for submission shall be as determined by the Executive Committee of the 1922 Committee after consultation with the Board.
- Deselection will be triggered as a result of the leader losing a 'no confidence' vote amongst Conservative MPs. A vote of no confidence in the leader will be triggered by 15 per cent of MPs (whose identities will not be disclosed) writing to the Chairman of the 1922 Committee asking for such a vote to be held. If the leader wins the support of a simple majority of the parliamentary party in a vote of no confidence, no further vote shall be called for a period of twelve months of the date of the vote. A leader who fails to win the support of a simple majority of those actually voting in a vote of no confidence shall resign and will be unable to stand in the election which follows.
- Nominations for the leadership will be invited by the Chairman of the 1922 Committee and a vote will be held by the parliamentary party. Votes will continue to be held by the parliamentary party in order to reduce the number of candidates to two. There will be no provision for additional candidates to enter after the first round of balloting.
- Once MPs have narrowed the field of candidates, party members will elect the leader on the basis of one member one vote.

There will be one member one vote for the selection of the leader of the Conservative Party. However, the parliamentary party retains a crucial role. On the other hand, the selection procedure will allow Conservative Party leaders to claim a mandate from the whole of the party, a useful weapon when dealing with parliamentary dissent. The deselection procedure may discourage challenges to the leader. Ballots involving up to half a million members across the country are harder to organise, and take longer, than those confined to a few hundred MPs at Westminster. Since the Labour Party changed its procedure from MPs only in 1981 its leader has been challenged only once, whereas Conservative Party leaders were challenged three times in six years from 1989 to 1995 under its MPs–only procedure (Kelly, 1998a).

The Labour Party

- In the selection for leader, each nomination must be supported by 12.5 per cent of the Labour MPs); where there is a challenge to the leader, any nomination must be supported by 20 per cent of the MPs.
- When the party is in opposition, the selection of the leader takes place at each annual session of party conference; when the party is in government, a selection shall proceed only if requested by a majority of party conference.
- Voting is conducted on the basis of an electoral college, giving one third of the votes each to:

1 **MPs and MEPs.** Each such member is entitled to one vote.

2 **Individual members of the party** on the basis of one member one vote. This ballot takes place on a national basis and is counted and recorded as an aggregate vote broken down by constituency party.

3 **Members of affiliated organisations** (overwhelmingly trade unionists) who have indicated their support for the Labour Party and that they are not members or supporters of any other party or otherwise ineligible to be members of the Labour Party. Voting takes place on a one–person–one–vote basis recorded by affiliated organisations and aggregated for a national total. The ballot proper provides for the declaration of support and eligibility required if no prior declaration has been made.

Voting in each section of the electoral college is on the basis of one member one vote (OMOV). The first leadership selection held under this procedure, in 1994, was the biggest ballot ever organised by a UK political party, with over 4 million members eligible to vote (see Table 8).

Table 8: *Choosing Labour's leader, 1994: the mechanics*
Candidates seek nomination from 12.5% of PLP[a]
↓
Electoral college[b] **PLP** (271 MPs and 62 MEPs) One third of votes: each member's vote=0.1% of electoral college **CLPs** (260,039 constituency members) One third of votes: each member's vote=0.0013% of electoral college **Levy-payers** (4.1 m. members from 38 affiliated unions and 12 socialist societies) One third of votes: each member's vote=0.000008% of electoral college[c]
↕
Ballot papers dispatched, collected and counted by Electoral Reform Society and Unity Balloting Services

Notes:
[a] When the electoral college was set up in 1981, a candidate needed only 5% backing from fellow MPs, raised to 20% after Benn's unpopular challenge to Kinnock in 1988. Complaints that the 20% figure precluded a desirable number of candidates in 1992 led to the 12.5% figure being approved at the 1993 conference. A challenge to an incumbent, however, still needs 20% PLP backing.

[b] Until 1993, the electoral college's composition had been 40% trade unions and 30% each for LP and CLPs, with block voting for the CLPs abolished in 1989 and for the unions in 1993. The 1994 contest was also the first in which union and CLP votes were aggregated nationally — no weight was attached to the result within one union, CLP or affiliated society.

[c] Following their conferences to discuss the contest, only a minority of unions (e.g. TGWU) recommended support for a particular candidate.

SOURCE: Kelly, 1997 (from Labour Party HQ). 'British Political Parties: Developments Since 1992' *Developments in Politics*, vol. 8.

However:

- most of the voters were levy–payers of affiliated trade unions with no direct involvement in the party.
- the procedure falls short of the OMOV ideal, for the votes of certain individuals are more valuable than others (see again Table 8). With each of the three sections of the electoral college carrying equal weight, the vote of someone in the MPs and MEPs section (333 members in 1994) naturally has more worth than that of someone in the individual members of the party section (260,039 members in 1994).
- the time, effort and cost demanded by the electoral college is enough to deter deselection of the leader. Over two months elapsed between John Smith's death and Blair's selection, in marked contrast to Wilson's challenge to Gaitskell in 1960 under the old MPs–only procedure, which took less than a fortnight. It was claimed that, by developing so much effort to an internal contest at a time when the Conservative government was most vulnerable, the Labour Party was distracted from being a full–time opposition, again in contrast to the leadership challenge in 1960 which caused only limited disruption to the party. There is also concern, especially among trade union leaders, about the cost of running the electoral college. In 1994, the Union of Construction, Allied Trades and Technicians (UCATT) estimated that a ballot of its relatively small qualifying membership of 130,000 would cost £70,000. It, and the National Union of Mineworkers, declared that they could not afford to conduct the national ballots required by the selection procedure. Thus, some 150,000 trade union political levy–payers were actually disfranchised (Alderman, 1998). The electoral college may, therefore, inhibit attempts to hold the leader democratically accountable.

The Liberal Democrat Party

- Candidates must be MPs, nominations proposed and seconded by other MPs and supported by 200 party members in aggregate in not less than 20 local parties (including the specified associated organisation or organisations representing youth and/or students).
- Deselection is called upon a vote of no confidence in the leader being passed by a majority of MPs; the receipt by the President of a requisition submitted by at least 75 local parties (including the specified associated organisations representing youth and students); the first anniversary of the preceding general election being reached without a selection being called, provided that the Federal Executive may postpone it for one year by a two–thirds majority and it shall not apply if the leader is a member of the government.
- Selection is by a one member one vote ballot of all party members.

The Liberal Democrat procedure is based on the purest form of one member one vote.

THE LEADER OF THE PARTY IN THE NATIONAL ASSEMBLY FOR WALES

The Conservative Party

These conditions may have changed by the time they are implemented, but at the time of writing they are as follows:

- Only members of the Conservative Group in the Welsh Assembly will participate at the first round stage. If more than one nomination is received a ballot amongst members in the Assembly will be held.
- Members of the Conservative Group in the Welsh Assembly may trigger a leadership deselection at any time but not less than 12 months after any previous selection. A valid nomination must receive the support of at least 15 per cent of the group membership or 3 group members *whichever* is the greater. Should the current leader receive two thirds or more of the votes cast he will be deemed elected.
- Should there be two nominations including the current leader and he receives less than two thirds of the votes cast, a ballot of the membership of the Welsh Conservative Party will be held. If more than two candidates are included the members of the Welsh Assembly and Welsh Electoral College will meet to consider each nomination and recommend two candidates for a ballot of party members in Wales. If only two candidates are nominated the ballot will be put directly to party members.

The Labour Party

- In the selection for leader, February 1999, candidates needed 2 nominations from each of CLPs; affiliated organisations; Assembly candidates/MPs/MEPs.
- Voting was conducted on the basis of an electoral college, giving one third of the votes each to selected Assembly candidates, MPs and MEPs; individual members of the party on the basis of one member one vote; affiliated organisations.
- The National Assembly Labour Group (NALG) Standing Orders, approved by the Welsh Labour Conference 1999, set out the interim provisions in case of a vacancy. It is conducted at a special joint meeting of the NALG and the Welsh Executive Committee (WEC) at which elected members of both are entitled to vote. The candidates are those Labour members of the Assembly Cabinet or Panel of shadows who accept nomination. When Alun Michael resigned as Labour leader in February 2000, the only candidate, Rhodri Morgan, was unanimously elected at the joint meeting of the NALG and the WEC.

Voting in the individual members of the party section took place on the basis of one member one vote. However, voting in the affiliated organisations section did not. Backbencher Rhodri Morgan won 64.35 per cent to 35.65 per cent of the vote of the individual members of the party. Alun Michael, the Secretary of State for Wales and Blair's favoured candidate, won the Assembly candidates, MPs and

MEPs section (58.43 per cent to 41.57 per cent). The decisive vote was delivered by the affiliated organisations section (63.96 per cent to 36.02 per cent). The Amalgamated Engineering and Electrical Union (AEEU), the General Municipal and Boilermakers Union (GMB) and the Transport and General Workers' Union (TGWU), which between them controlled almost 20 per cent of the total electoral college vote, did not ballot their members. George Wright, regional secretary of the TGWU, cast a block vote of his union for Michael even though independent polls showed that his members supported Morgan by two to one. One union that did ballot its members, Unison, split three to one in Morgan's favour.

THE CANDIDATE FOR GREATER LONDON MAYOR

The Conservative Party
- The Mayoral Selection Executive, comprising about 20 regional and area officers, all voluntary members of the party in London, nominates candidates.
- An electoral college, made up of the Mayoral Selection Executive, plus a representative from each of the 74 London constituency associations, meets to interview candidates and draw up a shortlist of three or four candidates.
- They progress to a 'hustings' meeting, at which every member of the party in London is entitled to attend and vote. Each member is able to vote for one candidate.
- The top two candidates from this meeting automatically go forward to the next and final stage, a postal ballot of all party members in London.

The procedure 'was designed to be democratic' (Michael Ancram, Chairman of the Conservative Party, 14 December 1999). However, when the Mayoral Selection Executive excluded Steven Norris on 11 December 1999, the electoral college asked the Mayoral Selection Executive to reconsider. The Mayoral Selection Executive called in the Board which reinstated Norris. As Ancram added, 'Democracy is sometimes untidy' (14 December 1999). There is only one member one vote for the final two stages of the procedure.

The Labour Party
- In the selection for London Mayoral candidate in February 2000, the London Selection Board drew up a shortlist. It was made up of 13 members as follows: four members from the NEC; four members from the London Regional Board; four independent members who were appointed by NEC and Regional Board members to the panel; the chair of the London Labour Party. A statement of candidates' qualities, setting out the qualities and standard against which candidates were measured included:

'1. Labour Party experience
Candidates should be able to demonstrate a record of relevant experience in the Labour Party, a commitment to its policies and programme and campaigns and elections. Candidates should be able to demonstrate their ability to work in partnership with a wide range of bodies'.

(London Mayor 3, Statement of Candidates Qualities for Greater London Mayoral Candidates, Greater London Regional Office, *The Labour Party*, 1999).

- Voting was conducted on the basis of an electoral college, giving one third of the votes each to MPs, MEPs and Greater London Authority (GLA) candidates; individual members of the party in Greater London on the basis of one member one vote; affiliated organisations.

On 16 November 1999, following more than four hours of debate at the Labour Party's Millbank HQ, the London Selection Board decided to adjourn and call back Ken Livingstone for a further interview. 'On the answers given, we could not be sufficiently assured on the commitment that Ken Livingstone has given us on his willingness to commit himself to the policies of the Labour Party and to stand on the party's manifesto', said the chairman, Clive Soley. Livingstone was finally allowed on to the Labour Party's shortlist on 18 November after agreeing to a 'loyalty pledge' to abide by the Labour Party manifesto for London.

Every party member in London, every trade union and socialist society affiliated to the London Labour Party and every London Labour MP, MEP and GLA candidate may have had 'the opportunity of selecting' the candidate for Mayor. (London Mayor 2, London Mayoral Selection Process — Procedural Rules, Greater London Regional Office, *The Labour Party*, 1999). However, it was not an equal opportunity. An electoral college in which over 60,000 party members in London got only a third of the vote, trade union and socialist societies a third, but the 57 London Labour MPs, four London MEPs and the 14 GLA candidates got a third was 'clearly unbalanced'. Each MP's vote was worth 'a thousand times more than that of a London Labour Party member' (Ken Livingstone, 'We're risking our chance of winning the mayoral race', *The Independent*, 13 October 1999). The Co-operative Party in London claimed just under a third of the vote of the affiliated organisations section, or 9 per cent of the vote of the electoral college. This was because of the fact that the Co-operative Party claimed 106,000 affiliated members in London. They were Co-operative society members who merely paid a £1 membership fee in a Co-op outlet which entitled them to a dividend on purchases. There were only around 1,700 actual party members ('How 14 people got to vote 50,000 times', *The Guardian*, 15 December 1999).

One member one vote for the party section of the electoral college may have encouraged 'maximum participation of party members' (London Mayor 2, London Mayoral Selection Process — Procedural Rules, Greater London

Regional Office, *The Labour Party*, 1999, p. 1). However, voting in the affiliated organisations section did not have to take place on a one–person–one–vote basis. For example, the AEEU did not ballot its members, casting its 50,000 or so votes, worth 3.9 per cent of the electoral college, via 73 union delegates, for Dobson; the 14-person Council of the Co-operative Wholesale Society of South London decided on the chairperson's casting vote that they would cast the 50,000 or so votes, worth 4 per cent of the electoral college, for Dobson. All of the nine trade unions who balloted their members recorded victories for Livingstone, some by big majorities.

The result was that, after the votes of the third candidate, Glenda Jackson, were redistributed, Dobson won with 51.5 per cent of the electoral college votes to Livingstone's 48.5 per cent. However, a total of about 80,000 people voted for Livingstone (including 21,082 individual members of the party and 10 MPs), compared to about 25,000 for Dobson (including 14,042 individual members of the party, 64 MPs, MEPs and GLA candidates).

SELECTION AND DESELECTION PROCEDURES FOR CANDIDATES

Following the introduction of proportional representation for elections to the European Parliament, the Scottish Parliament, the Welsh Assembly and the Greater London Assembly, there are different selection procedures at national, European, Scottish, Welsh and Greater London levels.

PARLIAMENTARY CANDIDATES

The Conservative Party

- A constituency association shall only adopt as its candidate a candidate whose name appears on the United Kingdom parliamentary list, established by the Committee on Candidates. In the case of a by–election, the Committee on Candidates may revise the List for the purposes of the by–election. The Board may, through the Committee on Candidates, from time to time publish mandatory rules as to the procedure by which constituency associations select candidates.
- The executive council of the constituency association establishes a candidate selection committee. Where there is no sitting MP, the Committee recommends not less than three candidates for interview by the executive council. Upon receipt of the recommended list, the executive council nominates not less than two candidates for consideration by a general meeting of the association which selects the candidate.
- A sitting MP wishing to seek re–adoption to stand again for Parliament is required to make a written application to the executive council. The MP has

the right to be heard by a general meeting of the association before any steps are taken to consider other candidates.

Constituency associations traditionally enjoyed autonomy over both the selection and deselection of candidates. However:

- The principle that all candidates are drawn from the United Kingdom Parliamentary List has been affirmed.
- The selection of by-election candidates is no longer done just by the constituency associations concerned.
- The Ethics and Integrity Committee can decide upon any action for 'conduct bringing or likely to bring' the party into disrepute (see Appendix 2). Although the Constitution clearly states that conduct which consists solely of expressing disagreement with the policies of the party shall not constitute conduct likely to bring the party into disrepute, 'disrepute' is 'an ambiguous term' (Kelly, 1999c) which might stop re-selection of rebel MPs.

The Labour Party

- A parliamentary panel, established by the NEC from candidates who take part in training and assessment weekends organised on a regional, national and specialist (for example, women, black and asian, young labour) basis, is brought up to date from time to time as additional candidates emerge from the process. Candidates recommended by nationally affiliated organisations through their own processes are automatically on the parliamentary panel. There are special arrangements made for by-elections and other cases where selections arise unexpectedly.
- Members of the national panel and other potential nominees are invited to indicate an interest in seeking selection by submitting an application for a particular constituency.
- Party units and affiliated branches may make nominations from amongst those who have expressed an interest to the CLP general committee (GC) for consideration. Where party branches nominate they are obliged to submit the names of one man and one woman. Other party units and affiliated branches may nominate one man and one woman if they so wish. In any constituency where one or more black or asian members of the national panel express an interest in selection the CLP executive meets to make a nomination from amongst those interested members to ensure that at least one black or asian candidate is available for short–listing.
- The GC invites all those nominated by party units and affiliated branches to a gathering to allow GC delegates to meet them; the GC draw up their short–list. Any sitting MP is automatically included on the short–list if they choose to contest the seat and are nominated. Where no sitting Labour MP is contesting the seat there shall be an equal number of men and women on the short–list. If four or more are nominated there has to be a minimum of four on any shortlist (i.e. at least two men and two women). There are separate ballots

between men and women candidates to determine which candidates are included on the short–list.

- Members of the CLP who are able to do so must attend a hustings meeting to hear the short–listed nominees before casting their votes. Any member may apply for a postal vote, postal votes only being granted to those who are unable to attend, not to those who choose not to attend.
- Where successful candidates are not members of the national panel there is an endorsement interview in each case before a recommendation is made to the NEC. For new selections it is carried out by an NEC selections board — or regional nominees of that board. The NEC selections board only interviews sitting MPs following a referral from the Whips office (MPs thus in effect are treated as members of the national panel providing they are not subject to a Whip's report).
- The Chief Whip presents a report to the NEC detailing unauthorised absences, abstentions and votes against the Whip of all members of the PLP and may recommend to the NEC that they interview MPs with exceptionally poor records prior to endorsement. This information is made available to their constituency parties. The constituency party meeting discusses the merits of the MP for a period of up to 30 minutes. They then vote on whether he or she should be reselected as the party candidate.

The procedure is underpinned by the principles that it should provide for 'the maximum membership involvement' and 'quality and diversity of selected candidates' ('Labour's future keeping a strong voice in Parliament', the *Labour Party*, 1998b). However, the freedom of CLPs is controlled.

- The national panel may be used as a way of controlling entry to the selection process. Although CLPs are not compelled to choose only candidates on the panel, where successful candidates are not members of the national panel there is an endorsement interview in each case before a recommendation is made to the NEC.
- Party branches are obliged to nominate one man and one woman, and a CLP Executive required to nominate a black or asian candidate in certain circumstances. A CLP General Committee has to provide for an equal number of men and women on the short–list in new selections.

The Liberal Democrat Party
- Each state party establishes a Candidates Committee to make provision for there to be a list of approved candidates for Parliamentary elections. In deciding whether to enter an applicant on the list, each State Candidates Committee takes into account the need to ensure that the list contains a reasonable balance between both sexes and different age groups, and includes representatives of different social and economic groups and of ethnic minorities.
- Short–listing is carried out by the executive committee of the local party or by a short listing sub–committee appointed by it. Subject to there being a

sufficient number of applicants of each sex, shortlists of two to four must include at least one member of each sex and shortlists of five or more must include at least two members of each sex; there must also be 'due regard for representation of ethnic minorities'.

- The local party arranges one or more hustings meetings at which all shortlisted candidates are invited to speak and answer questions. The electorate for selection are the members of the local party. Ballot papers are distributed to the members present at hustings meetings and are also delivered to members who submit a request, subject to such members being responsible for their return before or at the last hustings meeting.
- The requirements of the second stage of the procedure may be modified so far as necessary to accelerate selection if a general or by–election has been called or appears likely to be called in the near future.
- If a sitting MP indicates a wish to stand at the next general election a general meeting of the local party is called and, if the MP is endorsed at the meeting by a majority of those members present and voting by secret ballot, the member is thereby reselected; if the resolution is defeated, the MP may request a ballot of all members of the local party, and is reselected if the proposition is supported by a majority of those voting.

Candidates are selected on the basis of one member one vote. However, even the Liberal Democrats have an approved list for parliamentary candidates. A dose of positive discrimination is also introduced to ensure that the party's commitment to equal opportunities is demonstrated.

EUROPEAN PARLIAMENTARY CANDIDATES

Following the introduction of proportional representation for elections to the European Parliament in 1999, a new procedure for the selection of candidates was required. The new electoral system is a party list system (see Robinson, 1998). Under it, MEPs are elected from regional lists, rather than representing single member constituencies. England is divided into nine regions, Scotland and Wales each form one region. The parties must draw up lists of candidates in each region, and decide the rank order of their candidates within the lists. Ranking of candidates determines which candidates are most likely to be elected for that party. It is especially important given the closed nature of the list system: electors can cast one vote either for a party or an independent candidate, not show a preference for any particular candidate on the party list.

The Conservative Party
- Candidates on the European Parliament List may apply to stand in any region.
- A regional Selection College was established comprising:

Westminster Constituency Chairmen; Chairmen of Euro-Constituency Councils, which were based on the old first–past–the–post constituency boundaries an ceased to exist following the 1999 elections to the European Parliament; Area chairmen and Regional Co–ordinating Chairmen. The Selection College was chaired by the Regional Co–ordinating Chairman. The College undertakes its work in two phases. First, it meets to review the applications, discuss the requirements and process. At this first meeting a Screening Committee of around twenty (depending on the size of the region) is elected to select two and a half times the number of candidates required in the region to go forward for interview by the full College. Secondly, the selected candidates are invited to appear before the full Selection College. The interview process consists of a short speech followed by general questioning. At the end of the process a vote is taken to select a number of candidates to progress to the third stage. This should be at least the number required for the list plus 1 but no more than 1.5 times the number required for the list (rounded up). The Selection College ranks those candidates who have been interviewed but not put forward to the next stage so as to provide additional reserves for the final list.

The second stage of the selection process is open to any party member within a region. Its purpose is to select the candidates for the list and to rank them. A series of 'Rolling' Final Selection meetings open to all party members in the region is convened. All members present are entitled to vote for up to the number of candidates required for the list and for no fewer than 50 per cent (rounded up) of the number required. Members are required to vote for candidates in order of preference.

All the candidates have to come off the European Approved List. However, shortlisting is done by a 'fairly inclusive Regional Selection College comprising about 50 officials' (Kelly, 1999c). The ultimate decisions over selection and ranking are taken at a Final Selection Meeting open to all party members in the region concerned.

The Labour Party
The new procedure for selecting European parliamentary candidates, designed for the transitional year only, used existing European Constituency Labour Parties (ECLP's) as a basic unit in the selection process.

- Local party units could each make a nomination to the CLP General Committee (GC).
- The CLP holds a special GC meeting at which one man and one woman are chosen as the nominees from that constituency. Ballots for male and female nominees are held separately, with delegates entitled to vote for one man and one woman.
- All candidates who had successfully secured nominations from CLPs were then subject to a one member one vote (OMOV) ballot in the ECLP. The ballot paper was divided into two sections — for male and female candidates. At this stage the sitting MEP, where there was one, was subject to endorsement

through the ballot. Where sitting MEPs were seeking reselection for the 1999 elections, their name automatically appeared on the ballot paper in their own ECLP, in a separate section from that for new nominees. Members were simply asked 'Do you wish (name), your current MEP, to be re-selected as a candidate for the 1999 elections?' If the majority of members voted 'yes', the sitting MEP was guaranteed a position on a regional list of candidates. If the majority voted 'no' the sitting MEP was excluded from the remainder of the process and was not able to run as a Labour candidate. This process was called the trigger ballot.

- Candidates who had been nominated through the OMOV ballots at ECLP level were interviewed by 11 selection boards from Scotland, Wales and the nine English regions. These comprised five NEC members; three members from each Regional European Constituency, appointed by the London, Scottish and Welsh executives and specially convened European Regional Boards comprising members for the component party Regional Executives; one member of the National Trade Union Liaison Committee; one ethnic minority member appointed by the NEC; and the General Secretary. The selection board determined which nominee were shortlisted for selection from the national pool. All MEPs were automatically shortlisted.
- The final selection and ranking was done by a joint selection board. It ensured that there was 'at least one woman on each regional list' and, over the UK, sought to ensure 'a significant increase in the proportion of women Labour MEPs' and that women candidates were 'fairly represented at the top of regional lists'. The panel also sought to 'increase the number of black and Asian Labour MEPs.' ('NEC document DO/46a/3/98', *The Labour Party*, 1998).

The procedure involved 'all members through a one member one vote ballot', and candidates represented 'a range of backgrounds' ('Selecting Labour's European candidates for 1999', *The Labour Party*, April 1998). However, membership involvement was 'far from decisive' (Kelly, 1999c). It merely led to a reduced number of candidates being interviewed by a selection board of just 11 party officers, who then eliminated. The boards' own short lists were then reshuffled by a joint selection board which finally determined which candidates were placed on which regional lists and in which order. These two final stages of selection have been described as 'often an affront to party democracy' (Kelly, 1999c). For example, Christine Oddy, MEP for Coventry and North Warwickshire, was comfortably reselected by her ECLP, only for the joint selection board to rank her in an unwinnable seventh place on the East Midlands list of eight. With the MP having been critical of the Blair government, there was a suspicion that people had been pushed to the bottom of the list 'for political reasons rather than for their contribution in the past' (Diane Abbot, non–Blairite member of the NEC, 'Labour NEC deselects 11 of its MPs', *The Guardian*, 23

September 1998). Candidates 'represent a range of backgrounds', in particular with the proportion of women and the number of black or Asian candidates (*Selecting Labour's European candidates for 1999*, the Labour Party, April 1998). However, it can be argued that members' wishes are again 'constrained by the effects of positive discrimination' (Kelly, 1999c), with women candidates having to be chosen at both CLP and ECLP level.

SCOTTISH PARLIAMENTARY, WELSH ASSEMBLY AND GREATER LONDON ASSEMBLY CANDIDATES

The Scottish Parliament and the Welsh Assembly in 1999, the Greater London Assembly in 2000, were elected by a different form of proportional representation, namely the Additional Member System (see Robinson, 1998). This involves some members being elected in single–member constituencies under the first–past–the–post system, additional members being drawn from regional lists (8 in Scotland, 5 in Wales, 1 in Greater London). The lists are again closed party ones.

The Conservative Party

- The decision to admit candidates to the Panel of Approved Candidates in Scotland/Approved Assembly List in Wales was taken by the Scottish Conservative Candidates' Board (SCCB)/Candidate's Approval Committee.
- The selection of constituency candidates was conducted on the same basis as parliamentary selections. Each approved candidate was issued with a list of constituency association selection timetables and invited to apply directly to constituency associations.
- Only candidates selected by constituencies were entitled to submit themselves for placement on the Additional Members List by party members in the Scottish Parliament/Welsh Assembly region in which they have been chosen. The order of the Additional Members List is decided at a meeting of members in each of the regions following completion of the constituency selections.
- Those to be considered for the remaining places in each region must be approved candidates who have not been chosen by a constituency. These candidates are selected by the SCCB/Approval Committee.

The final choice of candidates for the single member constituencies was made by a general meeting of all association members. Candidates selected by the associations are allowed to appear on regional lists, thus ensuring that even those chosen to fight 'unwinnable' constituencies still have some chance of being elected. The ranking of the lists takes a 'reasonably democratic form' (Kelly, 1999c), being determined by meetings of members in the regions.

The Labour Party

- Candidates included on the national panel, controlled by the Scottish Executive Committee (SEC)/Wales Executive Committee (WEC), in conjunction with the NEC, sought nomination from party branch and affiliated organisations.

- In pursuance of the party's objective of 50/50 representation of men and women amongst Labour representatives in the Scottish Parliament/Welsh Assembly, the selections were carried out on the basis of twinned constituencies whose membership collectively formed the electorate for each selection.
- Party units and affiliated branches were able to nominate one man and one woman to the CLP General Committee.
- Each CLP GC then shortlisted at least one man and one woman but no more than four people in Scotland plus two men and two women in Wales.
- An OMOV ballot of members in the paired constituencies was then held. There are separate ballots for men and women candidates, members having one vote in each ballot.
- Each man and woman candidate who receive the highest vote and their representatives along with a representative of the SEC/WEC agree which constituency each candidate will contest.
- A special committee/council is established, comprising four members of the SEC/WEC, two NEC members, the Secretary of State for Scotland/Wales and the Scottish General Secretary/the party's Assistant General Secretary, to meet and discuss the composition and ranking of the regional list for each area. Within each electoral region, an electoral conference is convened consisting of three representatives from each of the CLPs concerned who are presented with a draft regional list submitted by the special committee/council. The electoral conference approves or refers back the regional list until agreement is reached on the same day.

The selection procedures for Greater London Assembly candidates were based on those used in Scotland and Wales.

The aims and principles of the selection procedure were to ensure the 'involvement of members including OMOV'; and 'to promote the diversity and quality of candidates', wishing 'to ensure a suitable gender balance' was included (London Labour Party Briefing, February 1999). However, the procedure was again prone to central control. In Scotland, Dennis Canavan, a prominent anti-Blairite MP, was among those excluded from the panel in what he said was a 'partial ideological cull'. Whips in the House of Commons supplied a list of 11 occasions when he abstained or voted against the Government since May 1997, and at his interview he was asked if he had ever posed any awkward or embarrassing questions in the House ('Left-wing rejects fight Labour 'cul''', *The Guardian*, 30 June 1998). The selections have to be carried out on the basis of twinned constituencies. For the selection of regional list candidates, the key body is the special committee/council comprising senior officials from the NEC and the SEC/WEC. Although the electoral conference, comprising CLP officials from each electoral region, approves or refers back the draft regional list submitted by the special committee/council, in practice it is the special committee/council which has the final say. For example, in Mid and West Wales the electoral conference referred back the regional list which ranked Alun Michael at its head, but the special council simply ignored this referral back and ratified its draft list.

POLICY MAKING PROCEDURES

According to Michels, political parties inevitably fall victim to what he termed the 'iron law of oligarchy', meaning that individuals who hold positions of authority within an organisation are not (and in the nature of things cannot be) controlled by those who hold subsidiary positions within the organisation. Michels identified two main groups of causes for this state of affairs, suggesting that there are both 'technical' and 'psychological' reasons for the strong oligarchic tendencies in all organisations. The 'technical' causes relate to what might be termed the inevitable division of labour within any large–scale organisation. Certain individuals must be accorded the right to act in the name of the mass membership, coming to devote most if not all of their time to the affairs of the organisation and becoming, in that sense, professional leaders. The 'psychological' causes relate to the widespread sense of need among members of a large organisation for direction and guidance.

McKenzie assessed the relevance of Michels' 'iron law of oligarchy' by examining the distribution of power within the Conservative and Labour Parties. He concluded:

'The distribution of power within British political parties is primarily a function of cabinet government and the British parliamentary system. So long as the parties accept this system of government effective decision–making authority will reside with the leadership groups thrown up by the parliamentary parties (of whom much the most important individual is the party leader); and they will exercise this authority so long as they retain the confidence of their respective parliamentary parties. The views of their organised supporters outside Parliament must inevitably be taken into account by the party leadership because of the importance of the role these supporters play in selecting candidates, raising funds, and promoting the cause of the party during elections. But, whatever the role granted in theory to the extra–parliamentary wings of the parties, in practice final authority rests in both parties with the parliamentary party and its leadership. In this fundamental respect the distribution of power within the two major parties is the same.'

(McKenzie, 1964)

In other words, that 'policy–making in both major parties was carried out in a broadly similar fashion, in that party leaders exercised formidable and unmatched influence — especially when in government' (Kelly, 1999a).

THE CONSERVATIVE PARTY

The Conservative Party's formal policy making procedure is a product of its Tory hierarchical ideology (see Chapter 4) and its intra–parliamentary structural origins (see pages 67–68). A study of policy–making in the Conservative Party begins with the sentence: 'Nothing becomes Conservative policy without the assent of the leader' (Barnes and Cockett, 1994).

However, it concludes that, although 'the leadership's role is pre–eminent', the leaders 'have always been prepared to modify their ideologies to accommodate the needs of government, the maintenance of party unity, or simply staying in power'. An examination of policy-making in the Conservative Party prior to 1955, undertaken by Seldon and Ball, shows that on issues like tariff reform in the early 1900s, trade union reform after 1926, rearmament in the 1930s, industrial policy in the late 1940s and housing in the early 1950s, the leadership's initial policy ideas had to be either dropped or radically amended in the face of pressure from both backbenchers and the extra–parliamentary party. (Ball; Barnes and Cokett; Kelly, 1994). This was done through informal pressure rather than organisational procedures.

More recently, there has been a change in the attitude of members of the Conservative Party which has had an impact upon policy making in the party. This change has eroded the deference customarily shown to the leadership. Both backbenchers and constituency activists are now less inhibited and, as a result, more likely to asset their own opinions. To understand this, it is necessary first to recall the embourgeoisement of society, both the cause and effect of the Conservative Party's electoral success after 1979. Instead of seeing themselves as an embattled and minority middle class, as they had done for most of the century, Conservatives became more inclined to see themselves as the new voice of the people, with a sure feel for the new, average voter. There was thus even less of a tendency to accept that the leadership 'knew best' when it came to policy. The party's long spell in office after 1979 also led to a feeling among many party members that they could now afford a much greater degree of dissent and free debate.

Parliamentary Party

It was already clear by the mid–1980s that a growing body of backbenchers was now prepared to question the leader's judgement on specific policy issues. The Thatcher governments discovered this on a range of issues, notably the reform of local government finance, Sunday trading and the funding of higher education (Norton, 1997). Once the government's large majority disappeared in 1992, rebellions became no less frequent and their impact more serious. This was demonstrated within weeks of the 1992 election when 69 Conservative MPs signed an early day motion calling for a 'fresh start' to the government's dealings over Europe. The division over Europe among Conservative MPs was to manifest itself in the government's ambiguous policy on the European single currency. Although the most important, the issue of Europe was not the only source of dissent among Conservative MPs. The government's plan to close 31 coal mines in October 1992 was recast after pressure from the Conservatives' trade and industry committee; dissent during the report stage of the Railways Bill led to an adjustment of policy in May 1993; and the privatisation of the Post Office was shelved after a threatened revolt in November 1994.

Party Conferences

It was not just dissent in Parliament which made Conservative policy embrace wider sections of Conservative opinion. From its establishment in 1867 as part of the new National Union it was made clear that the conference was to have 'no formal policy–making role' (Kelly, 1994). However, its influence upon policy normally occurs in oblique fashion. Any criticism of existing policy is seldon reflected in either the wording of motions or the eventual voting. Instead, conference goers have registered their views through the medium of free–range debate, often taking scant notice of the motion supposedly under discussion, with those on the platform trusted to sense and then cater for any clear views which emerge. For example, major revision of the government's poll tax policy, the decision not to 'phase in' the tax being forced on Nicholas Ridley by dissent from the floor at the 1987 conference, had nothing to do with the rather bland motion on local government which started the conference debate.

It would be wrong to examine the policy influence of Conservative Party conferences without reference to what Kelly calls 'the hidden system' (Kelly, 1989a). The main Conservative Conference each autumn is only the culmination of a series of Conservative conferences arranged throughout the year, one representing a 'hidden system' of 'grass–root influence inside the party' (Kelly, 1989b). This 'system' includes regional conferences, and 'sectional' conferences such as Conservative Women's conferences. These less publicised conferences provide further opportunities for ordinary party members to suggest policy. Some of these suggestions during the 1980s bore a strong similarity to eventual government policy. Most notably, the reform of married women's taxation in the 1988 budget echoed the results of questionnaires circulated at the 'Highflyers Conference' arranged by the Conservative Women's Organisation in 1986 (Kelly, 1989a).

Greater Involvement of Members

During the leadership contest in June 1997 Hague said that he would seek the endorsement of the whole party for his leadership. On 27 July he announced the details of that endorsement process. For the first time in the party's history 'each and every one' of its members would have a direct say, a vote, on the future of their party. At the end of September Hague would seek the endorsement of every member of the party both for his leadership and for his 'principles of reform' (see Appendix 1). They could back him or sack him. In 'an unprecedented exercise in

Conservative Party politics' (Kelly, 1998a), members were asked: 'Do you endorse William Hague as leader of the Conservative Party and the principles of reform he has outlined?'. When the results of the 'back me or sack me' ballot were announced at the party conference in October Hague and his principles of reform scored a more resounding victory than had once been expected. Of the 399,203 ballot papers sent out, 44 per cent were returned, 142,299 voting 'yes' and 34,092 voting 'no'.

A few days after the leadership election, Hague set up a task force to get on with the big changes that 'would have to take place' (Hague, 27 July 1997). That taskforce was led by Lord Parkinson, Chairman of the party, working with Michael Trend, Deputy Chairman of the party, and Archie Norman, Vice–Chairman of the party. John Taylor and Robin Hodgson in the National Union incorporated the work that they had already done on reform of the National Union into the work of that taskforce. Sir Archie Hamilton, Chairman of the 1922 Committee, and his colleagues on the Executive of the 1922 Committee, joined in that work and contributed their ideas.

The principles which Hague outlined in the speech on 23 July 1997 were the building blocks upon which the proposals in *Our Party-Blueprint for Change*, agreed by the working party under the chairmanship of Parkinson, and published at the party conference in October, were based.

Following the publication of *Blueprint for Change*, an intensive period of consultation took place. 22,000 copies of the document were circulated and around 150,000 executive summaries sent to party members. Every constituency association was asked to complete a detailed questionnaire. 405 of these were returned. 26 'roadshows' were held around the country which were attended by more than 3,000 party members. On almost every occasion the 'roadshow' team included a party officer, a National Union officer and an MP. At these events, proposals for reform were discussed in detail and a full account sent to the Reform and Renewal Working Party. 1,200 letters and feedback forms were received from individual party members, officers of associations and various party organisations. These were read by members of the Working Party team and considered as part of the consultation exercise.

The proposals produced in *The Fresh Future*, February 1998, took account of the ideas and suggestions that had been put forward over the previous three months. A number of changes had been made to the plans set out in *Blueprint for Change*. The reforms in *The Fresh Future* were put to the vote of every member of the party. Of approximately 330,000 ballot papers distributed, 116,185 (35 per cent) were returned, with 110,165 members voting 'yes'. This was overwhelming approval (96 per cent) of those who voted, but only 35 per cent of the party's estimated membership. the result of the ballot was announced at a Special Reform Convention on 28 March 1998.

The Fresh Future said that not only did party members expect to have the right to vote for the party leader and to be fully involved in the selection of parliamentary candidates, many also wanted more say in policy making. The party leader had promised that party members would be asked to approve the outline of the next general election manifesto and that the whole party would be invited to endorse the Shadow Cabinet's position on the European Single Currency. However, members must also have the right to be involved in the making of policy.

Conservative Policy Forum

Since its creation after the Second World War, the Conservative Political Centre (CPC) had played an important role in ensuring that those members who wished to do so had an opportunity to comment on policy and to learn more about the case for Conservatism. Its dual task of political education and the 'two way movement' of ideas between the party's leaders and its members remained as pressing as it had ever been. But there was a need to bring the CPC up–to–date and to ensure that all members of the party had the opportunity to be involved in its work. Therefore, the CPC was reformed and re-launched as the Conservative Policy Forum (CPF).

The principal functions of the CPF are:

- to encourage and co–ordinate the formulation and development of policy ideas and initiatives within the party, particularly the constituency associations;
- to establish a process for receiving such policy ideas and initiatives and ensuring a response is made to them;
- to consult by such means as it sees fit on such policy ideas and initiatives;
- to facilitate the development and organisation of high quality specialist input on important policy areas at a national level;
- to assist in the organisation of party conferences;
- to advise the leader and the Board of any policy ideas and initiatives so formulated and developed.

The Board appoints a Director of the CPF whose responsibilities include the formation of a structure to co–ordinate activities.

The CPF is managed by a Council constituted annually which consists of:

- a chairman, appointed by the leader, normally being a shadow spokesman (or in government, a minister);
- the Director of CPF;
- three elected representatives;
- a senior Director of the party, appointed by the Chairman of the Board;
- a representative from the Scottish Conservative and Unionist Party;
- up to five individuals with expertise in specific policy areas, co–opted by the Director of the CPF in consultation with the Council.

The CPF Council meets not less than twice every year with the leader to discuss policy ideas and initiatives, and membership opinion in relation thereto.

However, there are 'no *precise* details' of how members influence policy formulation, and how such influence is guaranteed, nor are there any provisions which '*compel* the leadership to heed the membership's view' (Kelly, 1998a). In short, members have, what the conference had in 1867, 'no formal policy–making role'.

THE LABOUR PARTY

The Labour Party's formal policy making procedure is a product of its egalitarian ideological tradition (see Chapter 4) and its extra–parliamentary structural origins (see page 71). According to the Labour Party Constitution, the work of the party is 'under the direction and control' of the party conference. It is the conference which decides 'what specific proposals of legislative, financial or administrative reform' should receive the general support of the party, and 'be promoted, as occasion may present itself', by the NEC and the Parliamentary Labour Party. It is the duty of every Parliamentary representative of the party to be guided by the decision of the meetings of such Parliamentary representatives, with a view to 'giving effect to the decisions' of the party conference. The object of the party is 'to give effect as far as may be practicable' to the principles from time to time approved by the party conference. The constitution also gives a clear role to conference in the construction of the party manifesto. Under Clause V of the constitution, the NEC and the parliamentary leadership decide which items from the party programme are included in the manifesto. Thus, conference sovereignty is clear. It appears 'the crucial, democratic link' in the Labour Party's policy making procedure (Kelly, 1999a).

However, the party's constitution exaggerates the role of the conference in the affairs of the Labour Party. Although the party's manifestos are supposed to contain only those policies approved by two–thirds of the conference, the leaders usually have enough weight to suppress the preferences of the NEC and insist that only the policies with which they feel happy go into the manifesto. Even if a party leader is obliged to accept certain policies in the manifesto he or she personally dislikes, there is no guarantee that those policies will be implemented should the Labour Party take office. The Labour Party constitution states that the object of the party is to give effect 'as far as may be practicable' to the principles from time to time approved by the party conference. It says nothing about the time and order in which manifesto policies are implemented, allowing the leadership to shelve the policies they dislike, often in favour of their own, prompted by events which were 'unforeseen at the time the manifesto was framed.

A number of policies were pursued by the Wilson governments of 1964–70 which either ignored or contradicted recent Conference decisions, for example devaluation of sterling and wage restraint. At one of the conferences during that period, Wilson told delegates that he regarded their decisions as 'warnings but not instructions', a 'rather odd interpretation of the Conference's constitutional role' (Kelly, 1989b).

The Labour Party was elected in 1974 on a manifesto whose objective was 'to bring about a fundamental and irreversible shift in the balance of wealth and power in favour of working people and their families' (Labour Party Manifesto October 1974), a policy endorsed by subsequent conference resolutions between 1975 and 1978. Yet from 1976 to 1979 the government emphasised the need for strict wage restraint, even after this had been questioned by conference, while agreeing to severe cuts in public spending in return for loans from the IMF, the terms of which were not discussed with the extra–parliamentary party. The government was restrained after 1977 by its lack of an overall majority, but the deals with the Liberal Party and the nationalist parties which ensured its survival were negotiated unilaterally by the leadership.

The leftward trend of conference decisions in the 1970s culminated in a radical party programme by the time of the 1979 general election. By then, the leadership was pursuing 'moderate' policies. In the event, Callaghan drew up his own manifesto with senior Cabinet colleagues, threatening resignation unless it was approved by the NEC.

The constitutional reforms inside the Labour Party between 1980 and 1981 were designed to check these oligarchic tendencies by making the parliamentary leadership more accountable to the extra–parliamentary party, notably through a widening of the franchise for the selection of the leader. However, the Labour Party's calamitous defeat at the 1983 general election served to underline one of McKenzie's justifications for an oligarchic approach to policy–making, namely that 'only a Westminster elite could be trusted to frame policies attuned to voters' wishes' (Kelly, 1999a).

After 1983, this was implicitly recognised by the new leader, Kinnock, and his closest associates in the Labour Party. Particularly after the Labour Party's third successive election defeat in 1987, there was a concerted attempt to centralise control over policy. The leadership kept a firm grip on the party's direction during the first stage of the 1987–89 policy review. The policy groups were dominated by key frontbench spokesmen and Kinnock used his position to make clear his preferences. For example, Kinnock's speeches and interviews were aimed at 'pre–empting the results' of the policy review, Kinnock using his television interviews, for instance, to voice his doubts about unilateralism (Garner, 1989). Although the review reports were not published until the middle of May 1989, the major provisions were well known before then. From the middle of March, Kinnock began a series of key–note speeches based on its findings. On the 9th of April, the Labour Party launched a two–month election campaign with a major rally in Birmingham in which the review took centre stage. Once again, as in the first stage of the process, the leadership was intent on 'pre-empting the final verdict of the party as a whole' (Garner, 1990).

The Blair Effect

Almost immediately after being selected leader in 1994, Blair launched a 6–month period of consultation within the party on the future of Clause IV of the party constitution. Questionnaires about Clause IV were sent out to individual and affiliated members, which made it 'the quantifiably largest single-issue consultation ever carried out inside a British political party' (Kelly, 1998b). Nearly 18,000 people took part in the exercise, an estimated 6 per cent of the membership. Of these, over 60 per cent agreed that the existing Clause IV was no longer an accurate expression of the Labour Party's objects. A new Clause IV was formally approved at a special Labour Party conference in April 1995 (see Table 9). Following the party conference in 1996, the party's draft manifesto was submitted to a ballot of all party members. This was conducted in October and November 1996, attracting a 95 per cent 'yes' vote and a 61 per cent turnout amongst individual members (see Table 10). A large number of affiliated organisations also balloted their membership. This was the first time that all party members had been directly consulted on the party's programme for government.

Table 9: *Labour Party ballot on the rewording of Clause IV, Special Labour Conference, 29 April 1995.*

Constituency party members (accorded 30% of votes)

Supporting proposal: 90%   Opposing proposal: 10%

Turnout: 41%

Affiliated trade unions (accorded 70% of votes)

Supporting proposal: 55%   Opposing proposal: 45%

(i) Unlike in the 1994 leadership contest, the constituency members' votes were cast by CLP conference delegates rather than by members themselves in a separate and inclusive ballot. However, about 500 of the 633 CLPs did conduct OMOV ballots before the conference, with turnout ranging from 91% in North Wiltshire to 24% in Nottingham East. In all these pre-conference ballots, a 'yes' vote was recorded, the highest majority being in West Worcestershire (97%), the lowest being in Leicester South (66%). The CLPs did not cast 'block' votes at the conference; instead their votes were split so as to reflect the minority as well as majority view.

(ii) The unions did not ballot their members beforehand, preferring instead various methods of 'consultation'.

(iii) The unions voting against change were TGWU, UNISON, RMT, GPMU, NUM, FBU, EPIU, BFAWU, ASLEF, UCATT.

Source: Kelly, 1998, p. 3.

Table 10: *Labour Party ballot on draft manifesto, November 1996.*		
INDIVIDUAL (CLP) MEMBERS		
Supporting the manifesto	218,023	(95%)
Opposing the manifesto	11,286	(5%)
Turnout:		*41%*
AFFILIATED (TRADE UNION) MEMBERS		
Supporting the manifesto	577,102	(92%)
Opposing the manifesto	50,182	(8%)
Turnout:		*24%*

Note: As with the 1994 leadership contest, all CLP members and all levy-paying members of affiliated unions were entitled to vote, with the votes aggregated nationally.

SOURCE: Kelly, 1998b, p. 4.

However, the manner in which Clause IV was reworded in 1995 and the ballot on the draft manifesto in November 1996 'seemed to represent an historic shift in Labour Party procedure', away from a participatory, representative democracy, in which a few thousand active members discuss in some detail, principally via party conferences, the ongoing development of party policy, towards a passive, plebiscitary democracy, in which hundreds of thousands of party members simply approve or reject policy packages assembled by a small number of senior parliamentarians and (often unelected) party officials' (Kelly, 1999a).

The National Policy Forum has the key role of overseeing a rolling programme of policy development. It has 175 members representing sections of the party, each elected for a two–year term with about half the forum elected each year. Policy commissions established by the forum are charged with preparing reports on the areas of policy under review. These are considered in detail and amended by the forum. The policy commissions are joint government/party bodies. Each is jointly convened by a minister/shadow minister and a member of the NEC, including equal numbers of representatives of the government/parliamentary committee (shadow government) and the NEC, significant representation of the forum itself along with representatives of the Parliamentary and European Parliamentary parties and local government. The National Policy Forum reports to the Joint Policy Committee, NEC and annual conference. The Joint Policy Committee is a steering group for the National Policy Forum, chaired by the leader with equal numbers from the NEC and government/parliamentary committee. ('Partnership in power', *The Labour Party*, 1997).

The aim may be to develop a policy making procedure which 'gives everyone an opportunity to participate', in which the policies presented to conference have emerged from 'an inclusive process of consultation and deliberation' (The leader's statement, National Executive Committee Report 1997, *The Labour Party*, 1997). However, the National Policy Forum usurps the conference policy–making role, 'giving conference little more than rubber-stamp status' (Kelly, 1997). Conference is apparently confined to either ratifying or rejecting the finished policy product, a clear sign to many that it has been changed from a serious, deliberative assembly into a 'rally' or 'celebration of new policies initiated by the leader and his or her advisers' (Kelly, 1999a).

THE LIBERAL DEMOCRACY PARTY

The Liberal Democrats' policy making procedure is a product of its liberal ideological tradition (see Chapter 4). Indeed, the preamble to the constitution declares: 'The Liberal Democrats exist to build and safeguard a fair, free and open society… we aim to disperse power, to foster diversity and nurture creativity'.

The defining characteristic of the Liberal Democrat policy making procedure is that formally 'Conference determines Party policy' ('Procedure for Policy Making', Policy Briefing 4, *Liberal Democrat Publications*, February 1999). Motions containing proposals for policy are submitted for debate at the conference by the Federal Policy Committee (FPC), local, regional and state parties and conference representatives. If conference accepts the suggestions, then they become formal party policy.

Development of policy on major topics is overseen by the FPC, which usually sets up working groups to examine the subjects in depth. Each working group produces an initial consultation paper outlining the main issues and areas of controversy. It circulates this widely inside and outside the party. After several months of meetings and consultations with experts and party members, the working group presents its proposals to the FPC in the form of a policy paper. After further amendment, this is submitted to the conference, which can amend any part of the policy paper, or ask the FPC to reconsider particular proposals. If conference approves, the policy paper becomes party policy.

The members of the Liberal Democrats play an important role in policy making within the party.

SUMMARY

The Conservative Party structure has changed, the three pillars of the old party–parliamentary, voluntary and professional — being drawn together in a single structure. The structure of the Labour Party is a natural produce of the party's genesis, confederal characteristics becoming a permanent feature. The Liberal Democrat party has a federal structure, comprising three 'state' parties, one each for Scotland, Wales and England.

Selection procedures for leaders of the Conservative Party are on the basis of one member one vote, but the parity leadership retain a crucial role. On the other hand, selection procedures allow Conservative Party leaders to claim a mandate from the whole of the party, a useful weapon when dealing with dissent. Deselection procedures, with ballots involving members being harder to organise, and taking longer than those confined to a few representatives, may discourage challenges to the leader. The selection procedure for the leader of the Labour Party is on the basis of one member one vote in each section of the electoral college. However, it falls short of the OMOV ideal, for the vote of an MP is worth more than that of a member in the other sections of the electoral college. Moreover, selection procedures for leaders of the party in Wales in February 1999 and Greater London in February 2000 did not have to take place on a one–person–one–vote basis in the affiliated organisations section of the electoral college. In addition, the time, effort and cost demanded by the electoral college is enough to deter deselection, therefore inhibiting attempts to hold leaders democratically accountable. Selection and deselection procedures for the leaders of the Liberal Democrats are based on the purist form of one member one vote.

Selection and deselection procedures for European Parliamentary, Scottish Parliamentary, Welsh Assembly and Greater London Assembly candidates in the Conservative Party are broadly democratic. However, for Parliamentary candidates they are less democratic. Selection and deselection procedures for candidates in the Labour Party are conducted on the basis of one member one vote. However, they are prone to central control, particularly for European Parliamentary, Scottish Parliamentary, Welsh Assembly and Greater London Assembly candidates. Selection and deselection procedures for Liberal Democrat candidates are conducted on the basis of one member one vote. However, even the Liberal Democrats have an approved list of candidates.

The Conservative Party's formal policy–making procedure is a product of its Tory hierarchical tradition and its intra–parliamentary structural origins. Members have no formal policy–making role. However, their influence upon policy normally occurs through informal pressure rather than organisational procedures. The Labour Party's formal policy–making procedure is a product of its egalitarian ideological tradition and its extra–parliamentary structural origins. According to the party constitution, the work of the party is 'under the direction and control' of the party conference. However, Labour Party procedure seems to have shifted away from a participatory, representative democracy, in which a few thousand active members discuss in some detail, principally via party conferences, the ongoing development of party policy, towards a passive, plebiscitary democracy, in which hundreds of thousands of party members simply approve or reject policy packages assembled by a small number of senior parliamentarians and (often unelected) party officials. Conference is apparently confined to either ratifying or rejecting the finished policy product, a clear sign to many that it has changed from a serious, deliberative assembly into a rally or celebration of new policies initiated by the leader and his or her advisers. The members of the Liberal Democrats play an important role in policy making within the party.

Revision hints

In terms of party structure, you should have knowledge of the parliamentary wing of each party, the professional bureaucracy and the party's mass membership organised at conferences.

Constitutional changes in the selection of party leaders should be examined together with the role of party headquarters and constituencies in the selection of candidates.

The study of policy–making should include the use of internal party ballots, such as Blair's victory in the replacement of Clause IV and Hague's victory in endorsing his position on the Euro. You might consider to what extent these exercises are genuine exercises in democracy and to what extent they are endorsements of the respective leaderships.

Exam hints

1 See question 1 (c) in Chapter 5.
   You should demonstrate a knowledge and understanding of the reforms to create a more unified party structure as proposed by William Hague.
2 How democratic are the selection and deselection procedures for party leaders? Demonstrate knowledge and understanding of the different selection and deselection procedures for leaders of the major parties, including the Conservative Party's two-stage process and the Labour Party's electoral college; also show an awareness of processes involving nomination requirements. Apply concepts and theories such as OMOV to analyse the extent to which the different procedures are democratic.

Practice Questions

1 To what extent are the selection and deselection procedures for party candidates democratic?
2 Does the mass membership of the parties play an influential role in policy making?

7

FINANCE AND MEMBERSHIP OF THE MAJOR PARTIES

Introduction

THIS CHAPTER WILL look at the funding of political parties in the United Kingdom. It will explain the sources of party income and discuss related issues, including whether there should be new state funding of political parties. Finally, it will examine the social characteristics, political activities and political attitudes of party members.

Key Points
- The sources of party income and related issues.
- New state funding of political parties.
- Social characteristics, political activities and political attitudes of party members.

FINANCE

EXPENDITURE

The Fifth Report of the Committee on Standards in Public Life, *The Funding of Political Parties* (the Neill Report), 1998, calculated that the Labour Party spent roughly £26 million on the 1997 election campaign while the Conservative Party spent roughly £28 million (Neill Committee, 1998). Many of the witnesses in their evidence to the committee made reference to the 'arms race', by which was meant 'a struggle between the two major parties to maximise income for electoral purposes' (Neill Committee, 1998). The increase in election expenditure is graphically demonstrated by Tables 11 and 12.

Table 11: *General Election Expenditure since 1983 (£M)**			
ELECTION YEAR	CONSERVATIVE	LABOUR	ALLIANCE/LIB DEM.
1983	3.6	2.2	1.9
1987	9.0	4.4	1.9
1992	11.2	10.2	1.8
1997	28.3	26.0	2.1
Total	**52.1**	**42.8**	**7.7**

*This table has been compiled from a variety of sources. Figures for the 1983, 1987 and 1992 general elections are drawn from David Butler and Dennis Kavanagh, *The British General Election of 1987*, Macmillan, 1998, p. 235, and *The British General Election of 1992*, Macmillan, 1992, p. 260. The figures for the 1997 general election have been provided by the three main parties in their submissions to us. (The parties also supplied figures for the 1992 election, but in our view the figures given by Butler and Kavanagh provide a better comparison.)

Table 11: *General Election Expenditure since 1983 at 1997 prices (£m)*						
ELECTION YEAR	CON. £M	PER CENT INCREASE/ DECREASE	LABOUR £M	PER CENT INCREASE/ DECREASE	ALLIANCE/ LIB DEM. £M	PER CENT INCREASE/ DECREASE
1983	6.6	–	4.0	–	3.5	–
1987	13.8	+109%	6.6	+65%	2.9	–17%
1992	12.7	–8%	11.2	+70%	2.0	–31%
1997	28.3	+123%	26.0	+132%	2.1	+5%
Total change 1983–97	**+21.7**	**+329%**	**+22.0**	**+550%**	**–1.4**	**40%**

SOURCE: Neill Committee, 1998, p. 43.

SOURCES OF INCOME

The Conservative Party

Personal donations account for an overwhelming percentage of the donation income of the Conservative Party. The remaining income comes from the constituency quota (the system of quota payments, which encourage constituencies to channel funds to the centre), and sundry income from conferences and sales.

The Labour Party

In 1998 40 per cent of the Labour Party's income was made up of members subscriptions and 'small donors'; 30 per cent came from the trade unions; 20 per cent from 'large donors'; and 10 per cent from commercial activity (Labour Party, 1999).

The Liberal Democrat Party

Between 1992 and 1997 the proportion of Liberal Democrat Party's income provided by members' subscriptions ranged from 30 to 66 per cent (Neill Committee, 1998).

PUBLIC FUNDING OF POLITICAL PARTIES

- Since 1975, opposition parties in Parliament have received public funds under a scheme generally known as **'Short money'**. Edward Short, the then Leader of the House of Commons, in speaking to the motion setting up the scheme, said that its purpose was 'to enable Opposition parties more effectively to fulfil their parliamentary duties'. Although it was the practice for opposition parties in the House of Commons to apportion some of the Short money to their respective teams in the House of Lords, in 1996 a scheme, known as **'Cranborne money'**, after Lord Cranborne, then Leader of the House of Lords, was introduced which provided funding direct to the first and second opposition parties in the House of Lords.
- Candidates at a parliamentary election, or an election to the European Parliament, to the Scottish Parliament, to the National Assembly for Wales and to the Northern Ireland Assembly, are entitled to **free postage** for one election communication to every elector in the constituency. Each candidate at these elections or a local government election is entitled, for the purpose of holding public meetings in furtherance of their candidatures, to **free rooms** in school premises or any other meeting room maintained by public funds.
- A further benefit to political parties (tough not one for which the state has to pay) is that the parties are given **free broadcasting air–time** both for party political broadcasts (which may take place at any time) and party election broadcasts. The parties themselves have to meet the cost of making the programmes.

TRENDS IN PARTY INCOME

There have been two principal developments:

1 *The re-emergence and growth of large personal donations.* In percentage terms, the Conservative Party is now far more reliant than it once was on non-institutional sources of income. For example, in the mid–1980s it was estimated that about 50 per cent of the party's income came from corporate sources. According to the party's accounts for 1996–97, that figure had fallen to around 20 per cent (Conservative Party Annual Report and Accounts, 31

March 1997). The Labour Party is also far more financially reliant on non–institutional sources of income than it used to be. There has been a proportional decline in support from the trade unions. The Labour Party told the Neill Committee in its written submission that between 1992 and 1996 the proportion of the party's income coming from trade unions fell from 66 per cent to 35 per cent, rising to 40 per cent in 1997 (Neill Committee, 1998).

In the six–year period from 1992 to 1997, the Labour Party received almost 300 donations of over £5,000, representing a third by value of all individual donations. Over the period 1992–97, the Conservative Party received over 1,300 donations of over £5,000. By comparison the Liberal Democrats received 100, the SNP 10, and Plaid Cymru none (Neill Committee, 1998).

2 *The development of commercial approaches to party fund–raising.* For example, the Labour Party has set up a 1,000 Club, where party members pledge to give £1,000 each year, and a High Value Donors Unit, with a small staff, who organise fundraising events to attract high value donors.

PUBLIC POLICY QUESTIONS

The principal questions which the Neill Committee thought arose in connection with party funding were:

1 The **misconduct** question. Do the ways in which political parties are funded cause ministers, opposition leaders and others to behave in ways that they ought not to behave? For example, do party donations by individuals, companies and trade unions, in effect, buy privileged access to ministers? Do they influence policy? Do they influence the awarding of contracts? Do they influence the awarding of honours?

Problems are perceived where the donor was (or could be) involved in policy discussions with the recipient party which became the part of government. An instance of this was the gift of £1 million by Bernie Ecclestone, the leading figure of Formula One motor racing, to the Labour Party. In November 1997 it was revealed that he had given £1 million to the party to help finance its May 1997 general election campaign. The disclosure came shortly after Ecclestone had had a meeting with the Prime Minister to discuss the exemption of motor racing from the ban on tobacco advertising at sporting events.

The Conservative Party received large foreign donations. For example, Michael Ashcroft, the large proportion of whose money was earned and banked abroad, gave around £1 million to the Conservative Party in the financial year 1999–2000. This major donation was made via the Belize Bank Trust Company (see Appendix 3).

2 The **fairness** question. The contentions underlying this question are (a) that some parties have much more to spend during elections than others, (b) that the fact that some parties have more to spend than others gives the former an electoral advantage and (c) that this advantage is, in some senses, unfair.

3 The **over-spending** question. Are the political parties simply spending far too much on election campaigns? Many feel, for example, that the scale and expense of modern campaigns is unacceptable because it offends voters and may thereby alienate them from the political process. Worse, the scale and expense of modern campaigns may also help to create, in a diffuse way, the impression that, irrespective of party, 'money talks', thereby further alienating the voting public.

4 The **civic engagement** (or the maximum participation) question. The argument here is that strong, healthy political parties are essential to the functioning of a strong, healthy democracy.

5 The **party effectiveness** question. This question relates to the parties' ability to perform their other principal functions, namely acting as a check on the government of the day (of whichever political party) and developing in opposition new ways of thinking about issues and new policies that are realistic and capable of being implemented in government.

6 The question of **freedom**. To what extent and at what point and with what justification is the state entitled to intervene to curtail freedom and rights of privacy in relation to the getting and spending of monies intended for the use of political parties? The Neill Committee proceeded on the basis that freedom should prevail save where they identified an overriding public interest calling for some limitation. They were totally satisfied that it was impossible to maintain all existing freedoms and at the same time to ensure that public concern about the funding of the parties was dissipated. The restrictions on freedom which they recommended were those which they believed to be essential to purify the funding of political parties. (Neill Committee, 1998).

THE CHANGING POLITICAL SCENE

There has been 'quite massive innovation' (Neill Committee, 1998) in connection with both the UK's political institutions and the methods of voting used.

- Resort has been made to referendums to ascertain the will of the people of Scotland, Wales, Northern Ireland and Greater London.
- In each case they have voted for the establishment of new institutions of government, a Parliament in Scotland, a National Assembly in Wales, an Assembly in Northern Ireland, a Greater London Authority and elected Mayor for London.
- In the case of elections to the European Parliament, a new system of proportional representation (Regional List System) was used in May 1999. For the Parliament in Scotland, the National Assembly in Wales and the Greater London Authority there was a new system of voting (Additional Member System). The voting system for the new Northern Ireland Assembly is by STV.

ARGUMENTS IN FAVOUR OF NEW STATE FUNDING

- It would 'purify' the political process. If there were state funding on a substantial scale, the parties would no longer be reliant upon large donors and, being no longer reliant upon them, would be immune — and would be seen to be immune — from any temptation to grant them privileged access to top politicians or unwarranted influence over policy, contracts or honours. Most of those to whom the Neill Committee spoke in Canada, Germany and Sweden considered that, whatever the disadvantages of state aid, the provision of it had the effect in their country of making the political process substantially cleaner than it would otherwise have been.

- Additional state aid would enable the parties to perform their functions more fully and effectively. In his evidence to the Neill Committee, Labour MP Martin Linton maintained that 'the parties were caught in a vice between falling incomes from traditional sources' and the 'rising costs of campaigning and the demand for more sophisticated policy research'. He warned that, without reform, we might see the development of either 'a slum democracy', in which the parties would be poorly staffed and unable to prepare themselves adequately for the task of running the country, or 'a sleaze democracy', in which the parties were 'forced into an unhealthy reliance on funding from private individuals' (Written submission to the Committee from Martin Linton, 27 February 1998). Some of those to whom the Neill Committee spoke also argued that increased state aid would have the virtue of signalling to the public that political parties are valuable, indeed essential, institutions in a democratic country.

- Paradoxically, state aid can be used as a means of increasing the involvement of private individuals in the political parties and in the financing of them. A number of countries, including Germany and the USA, use systems of 'matching funding' under which citizens are encouraged to give money to the parties in the knowledge that their individual contributions will be wholly or partly matched by the state or, alternatively, in which the parties themselves are given an incentive to raise money in the knowledge that whatever they raise will be wholly or partially matched by the state.

ARGUMENTS AGAINST NEW STATE FUNDING

- Taxpayers should not be compelled to contribute to the support of political parties with whose outlook and policies they strongly disagree.
- It would cause an existing party system — any existing party system — to ossify, with the existing parties handsomely supported out of the public purse but with new parties finding that they had to struggle hard to break in. Certainly, any system of state funding based largely or exclusively on the level of parties' support at previous elections is liable to have that effect. The Neill

Committee were told in Sweden of one small party that was still receiving state aid even though it had ceased to be actively engaged in politics.

- The question of 'civic engagement'. If the political parties were to become reliant on state funding, they might be tempted — depending on the system adopted — to abandon the strenuous efforts that some of them now make to raise money at the grassroots (by means of raffles, whist drives, garden fetes and so on). Fund raising is one of the most common activities in which local party members engage; if they did not have to engage in it, they might become less active in the party overall. State funding also runs the risk that, since the state's money would almost inevitably be channelled through party headquarters, at whatever level, the power of party headquarters might be considerably increased.

- Such a development would make the parties, in effect, part of the state. Instead of representing the citizens the parties would be tempted to represent the state; they would, in effect, have been 'captured' by the state. At the very least, there would be the danger that that would become the public perception. On the continent of Europe there is talk of 'cartel parties', which use state funding and the state apparatus increasingly to further their own ends rather than those of the citizens they claim to represent.

- There are two other arguments against any substantial increase in state funding. One is that the public would be unhappy about the prospect of state funding of the parties (a view unproven but almost certainly true). The other is that 'the needs of political parties are not the greatest priority in terms of public expenditure'.

THE NEILL COMMITTEE'S MAIN PROPOSALS FOR REFORM OF PARTY FUNDING

Donations

- Public disclosure of donations (including benefits in kind) to political parties of £5,000 or more nationally and of £1,000 or more in a constituency in any one financial year, from any one person or source.
- An end to blind trusts.
- Donations to political parties to be allowed only from a 'permissible source' (defined so as effectively to ban foreign donations):

'As to individuals:	registered UK votes and those entitled to register as UK voters
As to corporations:	companies incorporated in the United Kingdom
As to partnerships:	partnerships based in and having their principal sphere of operations in the United Kingdom
As to trade unions:	trade unions registered here pursuant to statute
As to other organisations:	organisations, voluntary associations and trusts etc. genuinely based in and having their principal

sphere of operations in the United Kingdom (but excluding branches of foreign organisations of whatever character)'.

- A ban on anonymous donations to political parties in excess of £50.
- Shareholder consent for company donations.

Limits on Campaign Expenditure

- A limit do £20 million on national campaign expenditure in a general election (including benefits in kind) by a political party.
- Clear rules on the preparation and auditing of a political party's annual accounts and national expenditure on an election.
- Controls on the activities of organisations and individuals (other than a political party) spending more than £25,000 nationally on political activity during a general election, with registration and reporting requirements, a ban on foreign donations and both national and local expenditure limits.

Public funding of Political Parties

- No new state funding, but tax relief on donations up to £500, to encourage small donations to political parties.
- A review of the arrangements for financing opposition parties in the House of Commons and House of Lords, with a recommended increase in funding to enable them to discharge their roles more effectively.
- Maintenance of free access to TV and radio for party broadcasts.

The Honours system

- Wider scrutiny by an Honours Scrutiny Committee of all proposals where there might be or be perceived to be a connection between the honour and a political donation.

The Media and Advertising

- Maintenance of the ban on political advertising on television and radio.

The Electoral Commission

- To ensure compliance, the system to be overseen by an independent and authoritative Election Commission with widespread executive and investigative powers.

THE BLAIR GOVERNMENT'S PROPOSALS FOR LEGISLATION ON THE FUNDING OF POLITICAL PARTIES

The White Paper on *The Funding of Political Parties in the United Kingdom* (July 1999) accepted almost in full the Neill Committee's recommendations. Exceptions were:

- Permissible source defined to cover only individuals 'registered to vote in the United Kingdom'; 'companies incorporated in the European Union and carrying on business in the United Kingdom'.

- Tax relief: the government was not persuaded by this recommendation. Tax relief would 'amount to general state aid by another route'. A tax–relief scheme would be expensive for the Inland Revenue and political parties to administer relative to the likely level of take–up. Furthermore, the government had to balance the loss of revenue (likely to be upwards of £4 or £5 million a year) against other spending priorities.

MEMBERSHIP

THE CONSERVATIVE PARTY

In the early 1950s membership was estimated at about 2.5 million; in the early 1970s about 1.5 million; by the end of the century about 335,000, according to a leak from CCO, and some think that exaggerated (Seyd and Whitely, 'Middle-class Activists' *Guardian*, Oct. 5 1999).

Social Characteristics of Conservative Party Membership
The latest survey of Conservative Party membership is one Whitely, Seyd and Richardson did in 1992. As Table 13 shows, the Conservative Party's 'achilles heel' is members' age (Seyd and Whitely, 1999). Only 5 per cent were under 35, almost half was aged 66 or over and the average age was 62. Considering the average age of Conservative Party members, it is not surprising that only 12 per cent of members had degrees. Men and women belonged to the party in roughly equal numbers. The typical Conservative Party members was less working class than the typical Labour Party member, although not so much so as the typical Liberal Democrat member.

Table 13: *Socio-economic Characteristics of the Party Membership (percentages)*			
	LibDems 1999	Labour 1997	Cons 1992
Gender (N=2807)			
Male	55	61	51
Female	45	39	49
Age (N=2794)			
25 and under	2	4	1
26–35	5	13	4
36–45	11	20	11
46–55	23	23	17
56–65	22	16	24
66 and over	37	23	43
Mean age	58	51	62

	LIBDEMS 1999	LABOUR 1997	CONS 1992
Table 13: *Socio-economic Characteristics of the Party Membership (percentages)* (continued)			
Social Class (N=2556)			
Salariat	74	64	55
Routine non-manual	11	14	18
Petty bourgeoisie	7	2	13
Foreman and Technician	4	7	6
Working class	5	15	8
Education (N=2866)			
University/CNAA degree	42	34	12
Activity (N=2358)			
Full–time paid work	38	48	27
Part–time paid work	12	10	9
Retired	32	22	40
Full/part–time voluntary work	5	2	na
Looking after home	6	4	16

SOURCE: Seyd and Whitely, 1999.

Political Activities of Conservative Party Members

Age and relative lack of education meant that members were fairly inactive in comparison with the Liberal Democrats or members of the Labour Party. As Table 14 shows, about three–quarters of Conservative Party members did not work at all for the party in the average month. For most party members, membership meant donating money to the party and little else. That was the only activity undertaken occasionally or frequently by a majority of members (see page 74, Whitely, Seyd and Richardson, 1994). The second most popular activity was displaying election posters in a window, but even this activity was engaged in frequently by only 18 per cent.

Table 14: *Rates of Activism within the Party Organisation (percentages)*	
Attendance at a party meeting in previous year	
Not at all	68
Rarely (once or twice)	14
Occasionally (three to five times)	7
Frequently (more than five times)	11

Table 14: *Rates of Activism within the Party Organisation (percentages)* (continued)	
How active members consider themselves to be	
Very active	5
Fairly active	12
Not very active	35
Not active	48
Amount of time devoted to party activities in the average month	
None	77.8
Up to 5 hours	14.4
5–10 hours	4.1
10–20 hours	2.0
20–30 hours	0.7
30–40 hours	0.4
40+ hours	0.6
SOURCE: Whitely, Seyd and Richardson, 1994.	

Political Attitudes of Conservative Party Members

It seems clear from Table 15 that many Conservative Party members had One Nation Conservative views. Majorities of members favoured spending more on poverty (81 per cent, only 11 per cent disagreeing); spending more on the NHS (80 per cent, only 13 per cent disagreeing); and giving workers more say in the work-place (64 per cent, 22 per cent disagreeing).

INDICATOR	DEFINITELY SHOULD	PROBABLY SHOULD	DOESN'T MATTER	PROBABLY SHOULD NOT	DEFINITELY SHOULD NOT
Table 15: *Political Attitudes of Conservative Party Members*					
One Nationism					
Spend more on poverty	29	52	8	9	2
Spend more on the NHS	31	49	7	11	2
Give workers more say in the work–place	16	48	13	18	4
Neo-Liberalism					
Encourage private education	28	36	20	12	3
Encourage private medicine	17	35	16	26	7
Introduce stricter trade–union laws	27	38	12	20	3
Cut income tax	20	40	13	22	4
	STRONGLY AGREE	AGREE	NEITHER	DISAGREE	STRONGLY DISAGREE
Neo–Conservatism					
Reintroduce the death penalty	36	33	7	17	7
Encourage repatriation of immigrants	32	38	12	15	4
Resist further European integration	19	34	16	28	3
Abolish child benefit	7	13	12	53	15
Make abortion more difficult	12	21	19	35	13

SOURCE: Whitely, Seyd and Richardson, 1994, pp. 138–9.

There is also clear evidence that many Conservative Party members supported neo–liberalism. Majorities favoured introducing stricter trade union laws (65 per cent, 23 per cent disagreeing); encouraging private education (64 per cent, 15 per cent disagreeing); encouraging private medicine (52 per cent, 23 per cent disagreeing); and cutting income tax (60 per cent, 26 per cent disagreeing).

The distribution of opinions on neo–conservatism were more divided. There was strong support for the repatriation of immigrants (70 per cent, 19 per cent disagreeing) and reintroducing the death penalty (69 per cent, 24 per cent disagreeing); significant support for resisting further European integration (53 per cent, 31 per cent disagreeing); but much less support for restricting abortion (33 per cent, 48 per cent disagreeing); and little support for abolishing child benefit (20 per cent, 68 per cent disagreeing).

Overall, the Conservative Party members tended to be One Nation Tories, neo–liberal, and to some extent neo–conservative.

There are two broad factors which explain the slow motion collapse by which the Conservative Party fell from being three times larger than the Labour Party in the 1960s to being smaller and much less active. One involves long–term social trends the party could do little about. The other has to do with changes in politics, many of them set in train or reinforced by the Thatcher and Major governments.

1 Class dealignment (see Robinson, 1998), the decline of the rural economy and the rise of female participation in the workforce. The alignment between the middle class and the Conservative Party has weakened. Rural decline and the shift in agricultural policy–making to the European Union has loosened the link between the Conservative Party and rural Britain. With female participation in the workforce rising Conservative women, who ran the social side of party life which played a strong part in recruiting new members and sustaining the organisation, no longer have the time to devote to party affairs.

2 Between 1979 and 1992 there were no fewer than 50 separate acts of parliament affecting local authorities and the aim of virtually all of them was to remove powers. People who otherwise might have valued a career in local politics concluded that it was not worth participating. Incentives to participate were further reduced by the enormous losses sustained by the Conservative Party in local elections during these years. In 1979 the Conservative Party had more than 12,000 councillors in Britain, but by the time of the 1997 general election it was less than 4,000. This wiped out a large part of the key activist base. Another reason for declining membership was Thatcherism itself. Most of the membership of the Conservative Party admired Thatcher, but there were many One Nation Tories in the party (see pages 30–31, 111). Many of them quietly left the party as it shifted to the right in the Thatcher years.

THE LABOUR PARTY

Social Characteristics of Labour Party Membership
A national survey of Labour Party members conducted by Whitely and Seyd immediately after the 1997 general election showed that the middle class continued to dominate the membership (see again Table 13). Members were much more likely to be members of the salariat (64 per cent) than members of the working class (only 15 per cent). With an average age of 51 they were younger

than the Liberal Democrats and Conservatives, but not by much. Surprisingly, the Labour Party had the biggest gender bias compared with the Liberal Democrats and Conservatives, women forming only 39 per cent of the membership. Some 34 per cent of members were graduates, making the party better educated than the Conservative Party but no as well educated as the Liberal Democrats.

Comparisons between 'Old' and 'New' Labour Party Members

Whitely and Seyd compared 'New Labour' members, defined as members who joined after Blair became party leader in 1994, with 'Old Labour' members, that is members who joined before 1994.

New Labour members were slightly more working–class than Old Labour members. Some 17 per cent of the former were in working–class occupations, compared to 13 per cent of the latter (see Table 14). Not surprisingly, New Labour members were younger than their Old Labour counterparts. 25 per cent of them were under 35, compared with only 12 per cent of the Old Labour group. The average age difference between the two groups was six years, with New Labour averaging 48 and Old Labour 54 years of age. New Labour members were more likely to be male than Old Labour members. Because Old Labour members were more middle class than New Labour members, they were also more educated. Some 37 per cent of the Old Labour members were graduates, compared with only 30 per cent of the New Labour members.

Table 16: *Demographic Comparisons between 'Old' and 'New' Labour in 1997 (N=5,761)*		
	OLD LABOUR (59%)	NEW LABOUR (41%)
Social Class (N=2556)		
Salariat	67	60
Routine Non–Manual	12	13
Petty–Bourgeoisie	2	2
Foreman and Technician	7	8
Working Class	13	17
Age		
Under 18 years	1	4
22 up to 25 years	1	3
26 up to 35 years	10	18
36 up to 45 years	20	22
46 up to 55 years	26	21
56 up to 65 years	17	15
66 and over	25	17

Table 16: *Demographic Comparisons between 'Old' and 'New' Labour in 1997 (N=5,761)* (continued)		
	OLD LABOUR (59%)	NEW LABOUR (41%)
Gender		
Male	60	63
Female	40	37
Trade Union Member		
Yes	38	29
No	62	71
Professional Association Member		
Yes	20	18
No	80	82
Household Income		
Under £5,000	8	7
£5,000 to £10,000	24	28
£20,000 to £30,000	19	20
£30,000 to £40,000	12	12
£40,000 to £50,000	9	7
£50,000 to £60,000	5	5
£60,000 plus	7	5
Graduate Status		
Yes	37	30
No63	70	
Religiosity		
Not all religious	36	31
Not very religious	27	29
Somewhat religious	27	30
Very religious	10	11
Belongs to a Social Class?		
Yes	67	64
No	33	36
If Yes, which class?		
Middle Class	41	40
Working Class	58	58
Other	2	3
Parents class when respondent a teenager?		
Middle Class	26	28
Working Class	73	70
Other	1	2

Table 16: *Demographic Comparisons between 'Old' and 'New' Labour in 1997 (N=5,761)* (continued)		
	OLD LABOUR (59%)	NEW LABOUR (41%)
Strength of Partisanship		
Very Strong Labour	58	38
Fairly Strong Labour	37	53
Not Very Strong Labour	4	9
Not At All Strong Labour	1	1
SOURCE: Whitely and Seyd, 1998.		

It is noteworthy that many party members who would be classified as middle–class by the sociologists thought of themselves as working–class. This is a well known phenomenon which was also evident in the 1990 survey of Labour Party members by Seyd and Whitely. However, the tendency for 'objectively' middle–class members to believe that they are members of the working–class declined somewhat since the time of the earlier survey. In the 1990 survey, of those respondents who thought that they were members of a social class nearly 70 per cent thought that this was the working–class (1992). With regard to subjective social class there did not appear to be any significant difference between Old Labour and New Labour in 1997.

There was something of a tendency for members to perceive that they were upwardly mobile. 73 per cent of Old Labour thought that they lived in a working–class household when they were young, and 58 per cent thought of themselves as being working–class in 1997. Thus some 15 per cent perceived themselves to be upwardly mobile. In contrast, the equivalent figures for New Labour were 70 per cent and 58 per cent respectively, implying that 12 per cent perceived themselves as upwardly mobile. It is clearly not the case that New Labour members were more upwardly mobile than their Old Labour counterparts.

There is a marked difference between the strength of partisan attachments of the New Labour and Old Labour members. The latter were much more likely to be strongly attached to the party than the former. The previous research by Seyd and Whitely had shown that strength of attachment is an important factor in explaining why some members are active when others are not (1992). As Table 17 shows, strength of partisan attachments has clear implications for rates of activism within the party.

Table 17: *Rates of Activism among Old and New Labour Party Members*				
ACTIVITIES DURING THE ELECTION CAMPAIGN IN 1997				
	YES		NO	
Did Members:	*New*	*Old*	*New*	*Old*
Display an election poster?	72	82	28	18
Donate money to party election funds?	61	68	39	32
Help run a party election day committee room?	8	23	92	77
Drive voters to the polling station?	10	21	90	79
Take numbers at a polling station?	17	33	83	67
Remind voters on polling day to vote?	40	48	60	52
Attend the counting of votes?	7	15	93	85

Did Members:	**Not at all**		**Once**		**Twice**		**Three or more Occasions**	
	New	*Old*	*New*	*Old*	*New*	*Old*	*New*	*Old*
Telephone canvass voters	93	88	2	2	1	2	4	8
Canvass voters door-to-door	86	70	3	4	3	4	8	22
Help with a fund raising event	87	74	7	9	3	6	3	11
Deliver party leaflets	63	43	8	8	8	10	21	39
Attend a party rally	83	74	11	14	3	43	3	8
Help organise a street stall	95	88	2	4	1	2	2	6
Help with mailings	86	75	5	6	3	5	6	15
Help with telephone fund–raising	99	98	0	1	0	0	1	1

SOURCE: Whitely and Seyd, 1998.

Political Activities of Labour Party Members

In 1997, more than three quarters of Labour Party members displayed an election poster, and about one-third delivered election leaflets on three or more occasions (see Table 17). Just under two-thirds did not work at all for the party in the average month, compared with one half in 1992.

Comparisons between Old and New Labour Party Members

Activism rates for the two types of party member can be seen in Table 17, which examines the political activities of members during the 1997 general election campaign. It is strikingly clear that the New Labour members were less active, and in some cases quite a lot less active, than long-standing members. Moreover, this was true with respect to every category of activism, particularly election–related activities such as taking numbers at the polling stations, running a committee room, driving voters to the polls, and even displaying an election poster.

The second part of Table 17 probes activity rates during the election in more detail and it shows very clearly that the New Labour members were a lot less active than Old Labour members. This can most easily be seen in relation to the two right hand columns of the Table, which contain percentages of highly active party members. Old Labour members were nearly three times as likely to do a lot of door–to–door canvassing and twice as likely to be actively involved in telephone canvassing in comparison with New Labour. They were almost twice as likely to frequently deliver leaflets, and more than twice as likely to attend several party rallies. The largest difference of all relates to fund–raising events, the Old Labour members being nearly four times more likely to help with several fund–raising events than New Labour members.

At the other end of the scale in the second part of Table 17 it can be seen that New Labour members were invariably less active than Old Labour members. Again the biggest discrepancies relate to canvassing, delivering leaflets and attending party rallies. In every case New Labour members were more likely to do nothing when compared with Old Labour members.

While it is true, as Table 17 makes clear, that fewer New Labour members donated money to election funds than Old Labour members, when it came to the total amount of money donated to the party overall the pattern was reversed. The median amount given by New Labour members was £30, whereas the median amount given by Old Labour members was £20. Thus, although fewer New Labour members gave money to the party election fund, they nonetheless ended up giving more money to the party overall than Old Labour members.

These results strongly suggest that the Labour Party had been recruiting a new type of member. The 120,000 new members recruited between 1992 and 1997 general election campaigns meant that any decline in average levels of activism was offset by the fact that many more people became involved. However, 'if this trend continues, activism will weaken in the grassroots party, which will affect campaigns' (Whitely and Seyd, 'Blair's armchair support', *The Guardian*, 7 April 1998).

Many of the new members joined in response to the mobilisation campaign. They became 'mail order' members, giving money to the party, but doing little else. This type of membership is welcome from the point of view of fund–raising, but it raises real difficulties for the party in fighting and winning elections.

Political Attitudes of Labour Party Members
In 1997, Labour Party members had lost their desire to move further to the middle ground of politics, compared to seven years previously. Only 45 per cent

agreed or strongly agreed with this strategy in 1997, compared with 57 per cent in 1990 (see Table 18).

However, only 37 per cent agreed or strongly agreed with the proposition that 'the central question of British politics is the class struggle', compared with 66 per cent in 1990. Over nationalisation only 50 per cent agreed or strongly agreed that 'the public enterprises privatised by the Tories should be returned to the public sector', compared with 82 per cent in 1990, only 22 per cent strongly agreeing with the statement, compared with 45 per cent in 1990. 49 per cent preferred more nationalisation, compared with 71 per cent in 1990. While there was still a majority of members in favour of redistribution, it was clearly no longer an overwhelming majority. 67 per cent agreed or strongly agreed that 'income and wealth should be redistributed to ordinary working people', compared with 88 per cent in 1990. There were still significant majorities favouring extra spending to alleviate poverty and to improve the National Health Service, though not the overwhelming majorities of seven years previously. In 1997 60 per cent though that the government should definitely spend more money to get rid of poverty, compared with 89 per cent in 1990. 75 per cent thought that the government should definitely put more money into the National Health Service, compared with 94 per cent in 1990. Over defence spending only 35 per cent thought that the government definitely should spend less on defence, compared with 60 per cent in 1990.

Table 18: *Comparisons of 'Old' Labour and 'New' Labour in 1997*					
(*Old Labour*, **New Labour**)					
	STRONGLY AGREE	AGREE	NEITHER AGREE/ DISAGREE	DISAGREE	STRONGLY DISAGREE
The Labour government should fine the parents of juvenile delinquents as a way of curbing crime	*17*	*30*	*14*	*26*	*13*
	24	**35**	**12**	**22**	**7**
Life sentences should mean life	*23*	*28*	*15*	*26*	*8*
	33	**28**	**13**	**21**	**5**
People who break the law should be given stiffer sentences	*20*	*26*	*27*	*20*	*7*
	27	**31**	**23**	**15**	**4**
The Labour Party places more emphasis on its media image than it does on its principles	*13*	*30*	*19*	*31*	*7*
	5	**21**	**23**	**41**	**10**
Tony Blair will stick to his principles even if this means losing a general election	*8*	*28*	*21*	*31*	*12*
	10	**38**	**20**	**26**	**6**

Table 18: *Comparisons of 'Old' Labour and 'New' Labour in 1997* **(continued)**

(*Old Labour*, **New Labour**)

	STRONGLY AGREE	AGREE	NEITHER AGREE / DISAGREE	DISAGREE	STRONGLY DISAGREE
Trade unions should no longer be affiliated to the Labour Party	*3* **4**	*13* **20**	*16* **21**	*45* **41**	*23* **14**
The Labour government should discourage the growth of one–parent families	*10* **7**	*22* **18**	*24* **20**	*31* **36**	*13* **19**
Individuals should take responsibility for providing for themselves	*4* **6**	*31* **37**	*27* **24**	*30* **28**	*8* **6**
It is desirable to retain private health care independent of the National Health Service	*5* **6**	*17* **23**	*17* **22**	*28* **28**	*34* **21**
Everyone's taxes should go up to provide better old age pensions for all	*27* **21**	*45* **43**	*15* **19**	*11* **14**	*2* **3**

Table 18: *Labour Party Members' Attitudes in 1990 and 1997*

		STRONGLY AGREE	AGREE	NEITHER AGREE / DISAGREE	DISAGREE	STRONGLY DISAGREE
It is better for Britain when Trade Unions have little power *1997*	1990	4	10	13	45	29
	1997	*3*	*11*	*16*	*49*	*21*
	Old	*2*	*10*	*14*	*49*	*25*
	New	**3**	**13**	**19**	**48**	**21**
Labour should adjust its policies to capture the middle ground of *1997* politics	1990	19	38	10	22	11
	1997	*9*	*36*	*21*	*28*	*6*
	Old	*8*	*34*	*20*	*30*	*8*
	New	**10**	**39**	**21**	**26**	**4**
The production of goods and services is best left to the free market *1997*	1990	5	20	17	34	24
	1997	*4*	*23*	*22*	*39*	*13*
	Old	*3*	*20*	*20*	*41*	*16*
	New	**4**	**28**	**24**	**36**	**8**
Labour should resist further moves to integrate the European Union *1997*	1990	5	11	12	48	24
	1997	*5*	*11*	*13*	*47*	*24*
	Old	*4*	*10*	*12*	*49*	*25*
	New	**6**	**12**	**14**	**44**	**24**

Table 18: *Labour Party Members' Attitudes in 1990 and 1997* (continued)						
		STRONGLY AGREE	AGREE	NEITHER AGREE/ DISAGREE	DISAGREE	STRONGLY DISAGREE
High income tax makes	1990	13	22	11	38	16
people less willing to	1997	7	19	13	47	15
work hard 1997	Old	5	16	13	49	17
	New	8	22	13	46	11
Income and wealth should	1990	46	42	8	4	1
be redistributed to	1997	23	44	20	11	3
ordinary working 1997	Old	25	45	18	9	1
people	New	20	41	22	14	3
A problem with the Labour	1990	6	9	15	54	17
Party today is that	1997	6	14	21	48	12
the leader is too 1997	Old	8	18	21	43	10
powerful	New	3	9	19	55	14

SHOULD THE GOVERNMENT DO THE FOLLOWING?		DEFINITELY SHOULD	PROBABLY SHOULD	DOESN'T MATTER	PROBABLY SHOULD NOT	DEFINITELY SHOULD NOT
Get rid of private	1990	41	23	18	14	5
education	1997	27	27	22	18	6
1997	Old	31	28	21	16	4
	New	21	25	24	23	7
Spend more money to	1990	89	10	1	0	0
get rid of poverty	1997	60	35	2	3	1
1997	Old	64	32	2	2	0
	New	54	39	3	3	1
Put more money into the	1990	94	5	0	0	1
National Health Service	1997	75	23	1	1	0
1997	Old	77	21	1	1	0
	New	72	25	2	1	0
Reduce government	1990	6	15	6	29	44
spending generally	1997	5	26	10	37	23
1997	Old	4	22	9	38	27
	New	6	30	11	36	17
Spend less on defence	1990	60	26	3	7	5
	1997	35	38	8	15	4
1997	Old	39	37	8	13	3
	New	30	39	9	16	6

Table 18: *Labour Party Members' Attitudes in 1990 and 1997* (continued)				
				1997
Are you generally in favour of:	1990	*1997*	*Old*	*New*
More nationalisation of companies by government	71	*49*	*52*	**44**
More privatisation of companies by government	2	*4*	*4*	**5**
– or should things be left as they are now?	27	*47*	*44*	**51**

		STRONGLY AGREE	AGREE	NEITHER AGREE / DISAGREE	DISAGREE	STRONGLY DISAGREE
The party leadership	1990	10	29	17	39	5
doesn't pay a lot of	*1997*	7	28	24	38	3
attention to ordinary *1997*	*Old*	9	31	21	36	3
party members	**New**	**5**	**24**	**26**	**41**	**4**
The central question of	1990	28	38	14	16	3
British politics is the	*1997*	9	28	27	28	7
class struggle *1997*	*Old*	11	30	24	28	7
between labour	**New**	**7**	**26**	**30**	**29**	**8**
and capital						
The public enterprises	1990	45	37	10	7	1
privatised by the Tories	*1997*	22	28	22	21	7
should be returned *1997*	*Old*	23	29	22	20	6
to the public sector	**New**	**20**	**27**	**22**	**23**	**8**

SOURCE: Whitely and Seyd, 1998.

On trade unions, a large majority of Labour Party members continued to disagree with the proposition that 'It is better for Britain when Trade Unions have little power'. Most continued to disagree that production of goods and services is best left to the free market, and continued to be in favour of further European integration.

Whitely and Seyd followed up the 1997 survey with a survey of attitudes which showed that nearly 30 per cent of party members disapproved of the Blair government's record. Criticism of the government's performance could be found throughout the party irrespective of social characteristics or activism. Members were asked to name the most urgent problems facing the country before commenting on the government's performance. The frontrunners were health, unemployment, law and order and education. Asked to rate the government's performance on what they considered the most urgent of these, as much as a third thought performance was poor, and a further 39 per cent thought it was only 'fair'. Members were concerned that the key public spending priorities of health, education and welfare were not being fully addressed. One question asked: Suppose the government had to choose between three options: reducing taxes and spending less on health, education and social benefits; keeping taxes and spending on the services at the same level as now; and increasing taxes and spending more on health, education and social benefits. Only 1 per cent chose the first option, and no less than three-quarters chose the third ('A question of priorities' Whitely and Seyd, *The Guardian*, 27 September 1999).

Comparisons between Old and New Labour Party Members

In 1997, only 33 per cent of New Labour members agreed or strongly agreed that the 'central question of British politics is the class struggle', in comparison with 41 per cent of Old Labour members. 47 per cent of New Labour members agreed or strongly agreed with returning privatised industries to the public sector in comparison with 52 per cent of Old Labour members. 61 per cent of New Labour members were in favour of the redistribution of income and wealth in comparison with 70 per cent of Old Labour.

Other differences between Old and New Labour related to the role of the market, attitudes to private education, attitudes to government spending in general and to income tax. Some 32 per cent of New Labour members thought that production is best left to the free market, in comparison with only 23 per cent of Old Labour members; 21 per cent of New Labour members definitely wanted to get rid of private education, compared with 31 per cent of Old Labour members; 36 per cent of New Labour members wanted to 'reduce government spending generally' in comparison with 26 per cent of Old Labour members; and 30 per cent of New Labour members thought that 'high income tax makes people less willing to work hard' in comparison with 21 per cent of Old Labour members.

The first three items in Table 18 related to the Blair government's 'law and order' agenda which expressed concern over juvenile crime and prison sentences. It is clear that New Labour members were markedly more conservative than Old Labour members on these issues. Some 59 per cent of them favoured fining the parents of juvenile delinquents, compared with only 47 per cent of Old Labour members; 61 per cent of them thought that 'life sentences should mean life', compared with 51 per cent of Old Labour members; and 58 per cent favoured stiffer sentences for law-breakers compared with 46 per cent of Old Labour members.

The last four indicators in the first part of Table 18 relate to attitudes to social welfare, two of which were linked to contemporary debates about welfare dependency. More New Labour members supported the propositions that 'individuals should take responsibility for providing for themselves', and that 'private health care should be retained', and fewer supported the proposition that 'taxes should go up to provide better old age pensions'. The one exception to the pattern related to the proposition that 'the Labour government should discourage the growth of one–parent families; in this case New Labour members were less in agreement than Old Labour members.

THE LIBERAL DEMOCRAT PARTY

Social Characteristics of Liberal Democrat Membership

A national survey of Liberal Democrat membership conducted by Seyd and Whitely in 1999 showed that over half were men (see again Table 13). Members were relatively old, although not so old as members of the Conservative Party; their average age was 58, over half aged 56 and over. They were overwhelmingly middle–class. Three in four worked, or before they retired worked, in a salaried occupation. In contrast, only one in twenty worked, or before they retired worked, in a manual occupation. Not only were Liberal Democrats middle class, they were also highly educated with 42 per cent possessing university degrees. Considering the age of the average member, this was not a by–product of the expansion of higher education in recent years. The Liberal Democrats could claim to be the most highly educated of the three major parties.

Political Activities of Liberal Democrat Members

Research shows the educated middle class are more active in politics everywhere in the world because they have more motivation and resources in comparison with the working class (Seyd and Whitely, 'Middle-class activists', *The Guardian*, 20 September 1999). Only just over one-half of Liberal Democrats did not work at all for the party in the average month.

Political Attitudes of Liberal Democrat Members

Liberal Democrat members were rather conservative on many libertarian issues. For example, 57 per cent believed that the government should discourage the growth of one parent families; 55 per cent believed that censorship of films and magazines is 'necessary to uphold moral standards'; and 44 per cent were opposed to the legalisation of cannabis (31 per cent were in favour).

On classical liberal issues, 43 per cent of Liberal Democrat members believed that 'the production of goods and services is best left to the free market', 33 per cent disagreeing (see Table 19).

Table 19: *Members attitudes on moral issues (percentages)*					
ATTITUDE	STRONGLY AGREE	AGREE	NEITHER AGREE/ DISAGREE	DISAGREE	STRONGLY DISAGREE
Cannabis	7	24	25	28	16
Censorship	14	41	14	24	7
One–parent families	14	43	23	16	4
Homosexuality	8	11	20	35	27
Abortion	8	17	22	38	15

Table 19: *Members attitudes on moral issues (percentages)* (continued)
"The use of cannabis should be legal for all citizens" "Censorship of films and magazines is necessary to uphold moral standards" "The government should discourage the growth of one–parent families" "Homosexual relations are always wrong" "The government should make abortions more difficult to obtain"

Table 19: *Members attitudes on social democratic issues (percentages)*

ATTITUDE	DEFINITELY SHOULD	PROBABLY SHOULD	DOESN'T MATTER	PROBABLY SHOULD NOT	DEFINITELY SHOULD NOT
Eliminate poverty	33	54	5	7	1

	STRONGLY AGREE	AGREE	NEITHER AGREE/ DISAGREE	DISAGREE	STRONGLY DISAGREE
Income and wealth	7	39	32	19	3
Individual responsibility	7	51	26	15	1
Aid to Asia/Africa	17	45	21	14	4
Production/free market	5	38	24	29	4

"Suppose the government had to choose between the following three options. Which do you think it should choose?"

Reduce taxes and spend less on health, education and social benefits	1
Keep taxes and spending on these services at the same level as now	16
Increase taxes and spend more on health, education and social benefits	83

Statements:

"The government should spend more money to get rid of poverty"
"Income and wealth should be redistributed to ordinary working people"
"Individuals should take responsibility for providing for themselves"
"The government should give more aid to poor countries in Africa and Asia"
"The production of goods and services is best left to the free market".

SOURCE: Seyd and Whitely, 1999.

On New Liberal issues, members were clearly committed to the government spending more money to eliminate poverty. Almost nine out of ten members supported this position (see again Table 19). However, less support existed among members for the redistribution of income and wealth to ordinary working people; a plurality (46 per cent) agreed with the idea, but one–third were uncertain and one in five opposed the principle. Moreover, support for the notion of an active, if limited social democratic state, seemed to be undermined by members' support for the Thatcherite view that 'individuals should take responsibility for providing for themselves'.

Members' attitudes to the European Union were mixed (see Table 20). One in five members believed in the long–term policy of working for the formation of a 'single European government', only 6 per cent agreeing with leaving the European Union. However, 37 per cent were in favour of reducing the powers of the European Union. It can be seen in the second sub–table in Table 20 that over two–thirds of the members disagreed with any moves to resist further European integration, and a further two–thirds agreed with the introduction of a common European currency. It would be fair to conclude that, while the party membership was pro–European, a significant minority of members, about a third, were Euro–sceptics.

Table 20: *Members attitudes to the European Union (percentages)*					
Britain's long–term policy should be:					
Leave the European Union			6		
Stay in the EU and try to reduce its powers			37		
Leave things as they are			14		
Stay in the EU and try to increase its powers			24		
Work for the formation of a single European government			20		
ATTITUDE	STRONGLY AGREE	AGREE	NEITHER AGREE/ DISAGREE	DISAGREE	STRONGLY DISAGREE
Resist further moves to EU integration	6	12	13	41	28
Introduction of common European currency	28	38	13	12	9
Statements:					
"Liberal Democrats should resist further moves to integrate the European Union" "Britain should agree to the introduction of a common European currency"					
SOURCE: Seyd and Whitely, 1999.					

Attitudes of Liberal Democrat Members to the Labour and Conservative Parties

Asked to rank both parties and their leaders on a thermometer scale ranging from zero to one hundred, with a score of less than 50 reflecting a lack of sympathy and a score of over 50 reflecting a warmth, Liberal Democrats strongly disliked both the Conservative Party and its leader, Hague (see Table 21). By contrast, this was less true of the Labour Party and its leader, Blair. As can be seen in the table, members were fairly evenly divided in their attitude to the Labour Party and displayed a greater sense of warmth towards Blair.

Table 21: *Members attitudes to the Labour and Conservative Parties (percentages)*				
THERMOMETER SCORES:	LABOUR	BLAIR	CONSERVATIVE	HAGUE
0–40	42	38	94	92
50	20	17	4	5
60–100	38	45	2	3
Mean	45	49	15	15
ATTITUDE	STRONGLY AGREE	AGREE	NEITHER AGREE/ DISAGREE	DISAGREE	STRONGLY DISAGREE
Labour politicians cannot be trusted	9	23	32	31	4
Liberal Democrats should have maintained equidistance	9	29	18	39	5

Statements:

"Labour politicians cannot be trusted and Liberal Democrats should keep their distance"
"Liberal Democrats should have maintained the policy of equidistance between Labour and the Conservatives"

SOURCE: Seyd and Whitely, 1999.

Liberal Democrats did have some difficulty with the abandonment of the policy of equidistance between the Labour Party and the Conservative Party. A simple majority (44 per cent) disagreed with the statement that the policy of equidistance should have been maintained, but over one–third (38 per cent) agreed.

SUMMARY

The Conservative and Labour Parties told the Neill Committee that between them they spent some £54 million on the 1997 general election campaign.

Without doubt the parties' belief that elections can only be won by the expenditure (mainly on advertising) of vast sums of money has given rise to something of an arms race. This in turn has put enormous pressure on party fundraisers to devise innovative ways of attracting donations. The result has been the well–publicised, very large donations to both main political parties and also the development of strategies — such as the fundraising dinner attended by senior party figures — which together give credibility to accusations that money buys access to politicians.

It is a small step from the thought that money buys access (encouraged by some party fundraisers) to the widespread public perception that money can buy influence.

Among changes in political arrangements that have taken place recently are the Parliament in Scotland, the National Assembly for Wales, the Northern Ireland Assembly, the Greater London Authority and the elected Mayor for London;new voting systems for the Assemblies and Scottish Parliament and changes to voting arrangements for elections to the European Parliament. The Neill Committee's proposals for change, therefore, aimed to have the flexibility to meet changing demands. The most significant part of their philosophy depended on transparency. While they accepted transparency was of major importance, they did not believe that it was sufficient by itself.

Fundamental to their considerations was to ask how much money the political parties needed to raise and how far their proposals would affect the parties' ability to do so. Their starting point, from the information received from the parties, was that the parties had had no insuperable difficulty in raising the funds they needed, even with the escalating arms race, although the 1997 general election left both the Conservative and Labour parties in substantial debt.

The Neill Committee had little doubt that the effect of some of their recommendations would have an adverse influence on the parties' ability to raise money, but they also believed that other proposals would have a significant dampening effect on the need for the parties to spend money. Taken as a whole, therefore, they hoped that their proposals would not have a deleterious effect on the financial health of political parties.

Membership of the Conservative Party has dwindled in the past decades while members have been getting older and less active.

Labour Party members have shifted their attitudes on the basic ideological questions of class politics, nationalisation and redistribution. They are nonetheless concerned that they key public spending priorities of health, education and welfare are not being fully addressed.

Liberal Democrat membership is highly concentrated among the educated middle class. The task of the party leadership is to maintain a membership recruitment strategy which will provide it with the active community campaigners upon which much of the party's electoral successes have been built. On the other hand, the type of member it is likely to recruit may cause it some difficulties in positioning the party in such a way as to both exploit any anti–Labour sentiment among voters while at the same time remaining part of the 'progressive' constituency.

STUDY GUIDE

Make sure you know the sources of party income and are able to discuss related issues. You should consider the merits of the state fully funding political parties. Make sure you know the social characteristics, political activities and political attitudes of the membership of the major parties. You should be able to discuss their implications.

Exam hints

---

1 (a) What are the sources of party income?
   (b) Discuss the regulation of party finance.

Demonstrate knowledge and understanding of the financial dependence of the parties on donations. Analyse reforms for greater openness.

6 **'Slow collapse'** (Patrick Seyd and Paul Whitely, *The Guardian*, October 5, 1999)

   'A question of priorities' (Patrick Seyd and Paul Whitely, *The Guardian*, September 27, 1999)

   'Middle–class activists' (Patrick Seyd and Paul Whitely, *The Guardian*, 20 September, 1999)

   Discuss these descriptions of the membership of the Conservative, Labour and Liberal Democrat parties.

   Demonstrate knowledge and understanding of how membership of the Conservative Party has dwindled in the past decades while members have been getting older and inactive; how members of the Labour Party were concerned that the key spending priorities of health, education and welfare were not being fully addressed; and that Liberal Democrat members were overwhelmingly from the middle class, on average more active than members of the other parties. Analyse, evaluate and explain the significance of the descriptions of the parties.

Practice questions

---

1 Should there be new state funding of political parties?
2 How representative are members of the Conservative, Labour and Liberal Democrat parties of the electorate?

APPENDICES

APPENDIX 1: HAGUE'S SIX PRINCIPLES OF REFORM

1 Unity
'Of course we need to be united about our future programme and our political beliefs, but we also need to be united in our organisation and our structure.... From now on, we are going to be one Conservative Party.... We will have a single Party governed by a single new constitution'.

2 Decentralisation
'Far from diminishing the role of constituency associations, i see them as crucial building blocks, and I want to see their role enhanced'.

3 Democracy
'Members of the Conservative Party should be consulted to a much greater extent on the way in which the Party is run. When it comes to the policies on which we will fight the next election, I will want the approval not just of the Shadow Cabinet, not just of MPs, but nothing less than the approval of the whole membership.... Our members must also have a say in the most important decision of all — the election of the Leader'.

4 Involvement
'We need to communicate with our members and listen to their views. Sometimes, we will wish to ballot our members. That means we need to know who they are and where they live. And that means we must have a national membership of the Conservative Party.

5 Integrity
'... our constitution must protect the integrity of our Party. We will not tolerate individuals, be they Members of Parliament, councillors or anyone else, who, through gross misconduct, bring scorn upon the whole of our Party.... We need a properly constituted disciplinary committee, with established criteria for taking action'.

6 Openness
'... we must be open about our funding... in future years we will list the major donors to the Conservative Party.... We will publish new guidance later this years, and our intention is that in future years the Conservative Party will no longer accept foreign donations'.

(A speech by Hague, leader of the Conservative Party, addressing a meeting at Conservative Central Office on 23 July 1997).

APPENDIX 2: THE ETHICS AND INTEGRITY COMMITTEE OF THE CONSERVATIVE PARTY

The Ethics and Integrity Committee is appointed by the Board. Consisting of the Chairman of the National Conservative Convention and the Chairman of the 1922 Committee, it is chaired by a Queen's Counsel in private practice. It investigates all matters put to it by the Leader or the Board. If the conduct of any member or applicant for membership is such that the Leader or the Board (in his or its absolute discretion) has grounds for thinking, is (or may be) conduct bringing or likely to bring the party into disrepute, the Leader or Board refers the matter to the Ethics and Integrity Committee. Conduct which consists solely of expressing disagreement with the policies of the party shall not constitute conduct likely to bring the party into disrepute. The Committee 'shall refuse to entertain any case which it considers to be based on policy disputes'.

After reference of any matter to the Committee, the Board has power to suspend the membership of any member pending receipt of the Committee's finding. Once it has reported, the Board must publish the Committee's finding and implement any action which the Committee has determined, such action including the issuing of a written warning, the withdrawal of any of the rights of membership, the refusal of membership, and the suspension or expulsion from membership of the party of any member.

Any person who is investigated by the Committee has the right of appeal to a person appointed by the leader, the person being one who has held senior judicial office or is a senior lawyer.

The first reference of conduct bringing the party into disrepute was made by the leader, Hague, on November 22 1999, in the context of the resignation of Jeffrey (Lord) Archer as the party's London mayoral candidate on November 18.

It was based on the assurance given by Archer to the party chairman on June 22 1999 that there were 'no new, substantial and damaging allegations' which could be made against him which would merit referral to the committee. Archer's admission in November 1999, that he had procured the fabrications of a false alibi by Ted Francis in the form of a letter to Archer's solicitors for possible use in Archer's libel action against the Daily Star in 1987, was prompted by the prospect of his imminent disgrace by the public disclosure of conduct which had never before been revealed.

The Committee concluded that Archer had engaged in conduct which brought the party into disrepute and that he should be expelled from the party for five years. Its finding was published by the Board in February 2000 and action determined by the Committee implemented.

Sources: The Conservative Party (1998) *The Fresh Future*, Conservative Central Office; The Conservative Party (1998) *Constitution of the Conservative Party*,

Conservative Central Office; The Conservative Party (2000) *Report of the Ethics and Integrity Committee,* Conservative Central Office.

APPENDIX 3: CONSERVATIVE PARTY GUIDELINES ON OVERSEAS DONATIONS

1 **Individuals and Partnerships**
Donations can be accepted from individuals who are resident in the UK and/or in full time employment in the UK and/or those who are entitled to vote in parliamentary and/or local and European elections and/or a holder of a UK passport who may live abroad. Donations can be accepted from partnerships whose membership is comprised principally of such individuals.

2 **Companies**
Donations can be accepted from companies incorporated in the UK. No donations shall be accepted from any company incorporated outside the European Union unless its shareholders are comprised principally of such individuals and partnerships from whom donations can be accepted.
Donations from companies incorporated within the EU but outside the UK shall be accepted if the donor company has a substantial connection with the UK.

3 **Unincorporated Bodies**
Donations can be accepted from unincorporated bodies whose membership or beneficiaries are comprised principally of individuals from whom donations can be accepted.

Donations can be accepted from any Trust wherever incorporated if the receipts of the Trust are substantially from those whose direct donations would be accepted.

(Published November 23, 1999)

The Conservative Party guidelines used a broader definition of a permissible source than either the definition recommended by the Neill Committee (see pages 100–107) or the definition proposed by the Government in its White Paper of July 1999 (see pages 107–108).

- Donations could be accepted not only from individuals 'entitled to register as UK voters' (the Neill definition) but also from 'a holder of a UK passport who may live abroad'. Thus, donations could be accepted from Mr. Li Ka-Shing, Hong Kong Head of Hutchison Telecommunications, whom it was said gave £100,000 to the Conservative Party for the 1997 general election, who would not be 'entitled to register' as a UK voter.
- Donations could be accepted not only from companies 'incorporated in the European Union and carrying on business in the United Kingdom' (White Paper definition) but also for companies 'incorporated outside the European

Union' whose 'shareholders are comprised principally of such individuals and partnerships' from whom donations could be accepted. Moreover, donations from companies incorporated 'within the EU but outside the UK' should be accepted 'if the donor company has a substantial connection with the UK'.

- Donations could be accepted not only from 'an unincorporated association having its principal sphere of operation in the United Kingdom' (White Paper, paragraph 1.5, p. 6), but also from 'unincorporated bodies whose membership or beneficiaries are comprised principally of individuals' from whom donations could be accepted. Moreover, donations could be accepted from any trust wherever incorporated if the receipts of the trust were 'substantially' from those whose direct donations would be accepted.

The Conservative Party said on 24 November 1999 that Michael Ashcroft was listed on the overseas register in Maidenhead.

GLOSSARY

Additional Member System A proportional system of election under which some members are elected in single–member constituencies on a first–past–the–post basis, additional members being allocated on a proportional basis.

Adversary politics The argument that the swing of the electoral pendulum leads to damaging policy reversals.

Bill of rights A document that provides a legal definition of the rights of individuals in the relationships between them and the state.

Checks and balances Internal constraints upon government which break up or fragment government power.

Class alignment The alignment between social class and party choice.

Class dealignment Weakening of the alignment between social class and party choice.

Classical liberalism The belief in a minimal state, whose role is limited to the protection of individuals from each other.

Coalition government More than one party in government.

Communitarianism The belief that the community is the source of the individual's identity and values, and, as such, that the individual owes the community a debt of loyalty and consideration.

Constitutionalism A system of government according to rules which imposes limits on the government.

Democracy Rule by the people, or the power of the people.

Devolution The delegation of central government power without the giving up of sovereignty.

Dominant–party system A competitive party system dominated by a single major party that consequently enjoys a prolonged period of government power.

Electoral mandate The idea that a general election gives the elected government a mandate to put its policies into effect.

Executive The branch of government that 'executes', that is applies the law.

Federalism The division of sovereignty between two levels of government.

First–past–the–post electoral system An electoral system under which the candidates have to obtain more votes than the next placed candidate to be elected.

Legislature The branch of government that legislates, that is makes, law.

Multi–party system A party system characterised by competition amongst more than two parties reducing the chances of single–party government.

Neo–conservatism A traditional conservative defence of state authority.

Neo–liberalism A traditional liberal defence of the free economy.

New Liberalism Modern liberalism, committed to intervention by the state.

New Right A belief in the free economy and the strong state, the combination of neo–liberalism and neo–conservatism.

One–party system A party system in which a single party enjoys a monopoly of power through the exclusion of all other parties (by political or constitutional means).

Parliamentary system of government The political executive is not part of the legislature, is selected by the legislature, and can be removed by the legislature if the legislature withdraws its support.

Presidential system of government The political executive is not part of the legislature, but is directly elected by the electorate, and cannot be removed from office by the legislature.

Partisan alignment Voters aligning themselves with parties psychologically by thinking of themselves as party supporters.

Partisan dealignment A weakening of the extent, and strength, of party identification, that is of voters identifying themselves as party supporters.

Party government A system in which the two major parties offer the electorate a meaningful choice between rival programmes and alternative governments; the winning party is able to carry out its manifesto pledges without having to negotiate or compromise with coalition partners; responsibility is maintained by the government's accountability to the electorate through its mandate.

Party list system A proportional system of election under which members are elected from lists, drawn up and ranked by the political parties.

Party system The system of interactions resulting from inter–party competition.

Political party An organisation which aims to exercise government power by winning political office, typically adopting a broad focus, addressing each of the major areas of government policy.

Pressure group An organisation which seeks to exert influence from outside, rather than to win or exercise government power, typically having a narrow issue focus.

Proportional representation Any electoral system which produces representation in proportion to the votes cast.

Social democracy A form of socialism that stands for a balance between the market and the state.

Socialism An ideology characterised by a belief in community, cooperation, equality and common ownership.

Third way A modernised social democracy.

Toryism An ideological stance within conservatism characterised by a belief in hierarchy, an emphasis on tradition and support for duty and organicism.

Two–party system A party system in which only two parties enjoy sufficient electoral and legislative strength to have a realistic prospect of winning government power; the larger party is able to rule alone; and power alternates between these parties.

FURTHER READING AND RESOURCES

BOOKS

Abrams, M. and Rose, R. (1960) *Must Labour Lose?* Harmondsworth: Penguin
Alderman, K. (1999) 'Leadership Elections in the Conservative and Labour Parties', *Developments in Politics*, Vol. 9, pp. 5–73, Ormskirk: Causeway Press.
Ball, S. (1994) 'The National and Regional Party Structure', in Seldon, A. and Ball, S. (eds) *Conservative Century*, pp. 169–220, Oxford: Oxford University Press.
Barnes, J. and Cockett, R. (1994) 'The Making of Party Policy', in Seldon, A. and Ball S. (eds) *Conservative Century*, pp. 347–82, Oxford: Oxford University Press.

Blair, T. (1998) *The Third Way*, London: The Fabian Society.

Blake, R. (1997) *The Conservative Party from Peel to Major*, London: Arrow Books.

Brack, D. (1996) 'Liberal Democrat policy', in MacIver, D. (ed) *The Liberal Democrats*, pp. 85–110, Hemel Hempstead: Prentice Hall/Harvest Wheatsheaf.

Burke, E. (1975) *Reflections on the Revolution in France*, ed O'Brien, C. Harmondsworth: Penguin.

Butler, D. and Kavanagh, D. (1997) *The British General Election of 1997*, Basingstoke and London: Macmillan.

Conservative Party (1997) *A Fresh Future for the Conservative Party*, London: Conservative Central Office.

Conservative Party (1998a) *Constitution of the Conservative Party*, London: Conservative Central Office.

Conservative Party (1998b) *The Fresh Future*, London: Conservative Central Office.

Conservative Party (1999a) *Listening to Britain*, London: Conservative Central Office.

Conservative Party (1999b) *The Common Sense Revolution*, London: Conservative Central Office.

Crosland, A. (1956) *The Future of Socialism*, London: Jonathan Cape.

Crosland, A. (1974) *Socialism Now*, London: Jonathan Cape.

Cunningham, M. (1998) 'The Parties of Wales, Scotland and Northern Ireland' in Garner, R. and Kelly, R. *British Political Parties Today*, Manchester: Manchester University Press.

Curtice, J. and Steed, M. (1997) 'Appendix 2 The Results Analysed, in Butler, D. and Kavanagh, D. *The British General Election of 1997*, pp. 295–325, Basingstoke and London: Macmillan.

Etzioni, A. (1995) *The Spirit of Community: Rights, Responsibilities and the Communication Agenda*, London: Fontana.

Friedman, M. (1962) *Capitalism and Freedom*, Chicago, Ill.: University of Chicago Press.

Galbraith, J. (1992) *The Culture of Contentment*, London: Sinclair Stevenson.

Gamble, A. (1988) *The Free Market and the Strong State*, Basingstoke and London: Macmillan.

Garner, R. (1990) 'Labour and the Policy Review: A Party Fit to Govern?' *Talking Politics*, Vol. 3, No. 1, pp. 31–6,Manchester: The Politics Association.

Garner, R. and Kelly, R. (1998) *British Political Parties Today*, 2and edn, Manchester: Manchester University Press.

Giddens, A. (1998) *The Third Way*, Cambridge: Polity Press.

Gould, P. (1998) *The Unfinished Revolution*, London: Little, Brown and Company.

Grant, M. (1997) 'The Dog Days of John Major's Minority Government', *Talking Politics*, Vol. 10, No. 1, pp. 14–16, Manchester: The Politics Association.

Gray, J. (1996) *After Social Democracy: Politics, Capitalism and the Common Life*, London: Demos, 1996.

Gray, J. and Willets, D. (1997) *Is Conservatism Dead?* London: Profile Books.

Green, T. (1988) *Works*, ed Nettleship, R., London: Oxford University Press.

Gyford, J. (1994) 'Party Politics in Local Government', in Robins, L., Blackmore, H. and Pyper, R. *Britain's Changing Party System*, pp. 110–24, Leicester: Leicester University Press.

Hayek, F. (1960) *The Constitution of Liberty*, London: Routledge & Kegan Paul.

Hazell, R. (ed) (1999) *Constitutional Futures: A History of the Next Ten Years*, Oxford: Oxford University Press.

Heywood, A. (1993) 'The dominant-party system: a threat to democracy?' *Talking Politics*, Vol. 5, No. 2, pp. 85–9, Manchester: The Politics Association.

Heywood, A. (1994) 'Britain's dominant party system,' in Robins, L., Blackmore, H., and Pyper, R., *Britain's Changing Party System*, pp. 10–25, London: Leicester University Press.

Heywood, A. (1997) *Politics*, Basingstoke and London: Macmillan.

Heywood, A. (1998a) *Political Ideologies*, 2nd edn, Basingstoke and London: Macmillan.

Heywood, A. (1998b) 'It's the Culture Stupid–Deconstructing the Blair Project,' *Talking Politics*, Vol. 11, No. 1, pp. 42–6, Manchester: The Politics Association.

Hobhouse, L.T. (1942) *Liberalism*, Oxford: University Press.

Hutton, W. (1995) *The State We're In*, London: Jonathan Cape.

Kavanagh, D. (1997) *The Reordering of British Politics*, Oxford: Oxford University Press.

Kavanagh, D. and Morris, P. (1989) *Consensus Politics from Attlee to Thatcher*, Oxford: Basil Blackwell.

Kelly, R. (1989a) *Conservative Party Conferences*, Manchester: Manchester University Press.

Kelly, R. (1989b) 'Party Conferences: Do They Matter?' *Talking Politics*, Vol. 2, No. 1, pp. 2–5, Manchester: The Politics Association.

Kelly, R. (1994) 'The Party Conferences', in Seldon, A. and Ball, S. (eds) *Conservative Century*, pp. 221–60, Oxford: Oxford University Press.

Kelly, R. (1997) 'The Tory Way is the Better Way', *Political Quarterly*, Vol. 68, No. 3.

Kelly, R. (1998a) 'Democratising The Tory Party', *Talking Politics*, Vol. 11, No. 1, pp. 28–33, Manchester: The Politics Association.

Kelly, R. (1998b) 'Power in the Labour Party — The Blair Effect', *Politics Review*, Vol. 8, No. 2, pp. 2–6, Deddington: Philip Allan.

Kelly, R. (ed) (1999a) *Changing Party Policy in Britain*, Oxford: Blackwell.

Kelly, R. (1999b) 'Power in the Conservative Party', *Politics Review*, Vol. 8, No. 3, pp. 28–30, Deddington: Philip Allan.

Kelly, R. (1999c) 'Selecting Party Candidates', *Talking Politics*, Vol. 12, No. 1, pp. 222–7, Manchester: The Politics Association.

Keynes, J.M. (1965) *The General Theory of Employment, Interest and Money*, San Diego: Harcourt Brace Jovanovich.

King, A. (1976) 'The problem of overload', in King, A. (ed) *Why is Britain becoming harder to govern?* pp. 8–30, London: British Broadcasting Corporation.

Kircheimer, O. (1966) 'The Transformation of the Western European Party Systems', in Palombara, J. la and Weiner, M. (eds) *Political Parties and Political Development*, Princeton, N.J.: Princeton University Press.

Labour Party (1997) *Partnership in power*, London: Labour Party.

Labour Party (1998b) *Labour's future keeping a strong voice in Parliament*, London: Labour Party.

Labour Party (1998a) *National Executive Committee Paper*, 23 January, London: Labour Party.

Labour Party (1999) *Annual Report*, London: Labour Party.

Leach, R. (1998) 'Political Ideas', *Developments in Politics*, Vol. 9, pp. 28–50, Ormskirk: Causeway Press.

Lipow, A. and Seyd, P. (1996) 'the Politics of Anti-Partyism', *Parliamentary Affairs*, Vol. 49, No. 2, pp. 273–84, Oxford: Oxford University Press.

MacIntyre, A. (1981) *After Virtue*, Notre Dame, IL: University of Notre Dame Press.

McKenzie, R. (1964) *British Political Parties*, 2nd edn, London: Mercury Books.

Macmillan, H. (1966) *The Middle Way*, London: Macmillan.

Mill, J.S. (1982) *On Liberty*, Harmondsworth: Penguin.

Minkin, L. (1978) *The Labour Party Conference*, Manchester: Manchester University Press.

More, T. (1965) *Utopia*, trans. Turner, P., Harmondsworth: Penguin.

Neill Committee (1998) Fifth Report of the Committee on Standards in Public Life, *The Funding of Political Parties in the United Kingdom*, Cm 4057, London: The Stationary Office.

Norton, P. (1987) *Parliament in Perspective*, Hull: Hull University Press.

O'Connor, J. (1973) *The Fiscal Crisis of the Capitalist State*, New York: St. James' Press.

O'Leary, B. (1994) 'Britain's Japanese Question: "Is There a Dominant Party?"' in Margetts, H. and Smyth, G. *Turning Japanese? Britain with a Permanent Party of Government*, London: Lawrence & Wishart.

Plant, R. (1999) 'Crosland, Equality and New Labour', in Leonard, D. (ed) *Crosland and New Labour*, pp. 19–34, Basingstoke and London: Macmillan.

Plato (1955) *The Republic*, trans. Lee, H., Harmondsworth: Penguin.

Rawls, J. (1971) *A Theory of Justice*, Oxford: Oxford University Press.

Robins, L., Blackmore, H. and Pyper, R. (1994) *Britain's Changing Party System*, Leicester: Leicester University Press.

Robinson, C. (1998) *Voting Behaviour and Electoral Systems*, London: Hodder & Stoughton.

Rose, R. (1984) *Do Parties make a Difference?* 2nd edn, London and Basingstoke: Macmillan.

Sandel, M. (1982) *Liberalism and the Limits of Justice*, Cambridge: Cambridge University Press.

Sartori, G. (1976) *Parties and Party Systems: A Framework for Analysis*, Cambridge: Cambridge University Press.

Scruton, R. (1980) *The Meaning of Conservatism*, Harmondsworth: Penguin

Seldon, A. and Ball, S. (eds) (1994) *Conservative Century*, Oxford: Oxford University Press.

Seyd, P. (1998) 'In Praise of Party', *Parliamentary Affairs*, Vol. 51, No. 3, pp. 198–208, Oxford: Oxford University Press.

Seyd, P. and Whitely, P. (1995) 'Labour and Conservative Party Members: Change Over Time', *Parliamentary Affairs*, Vol. 48, No. 3, pp. 456–72, Oxford: Oxford University Press.

Seyd, P. and Whitely, P. (1999) *Liberal Democrats at the Grassroots Who Are They?* Sheffield: University of Sheffield.

Simpson, D. (1998) *UK Government and Politics in Context*, London: Hodder & Stoughton.

Simpson, D. (1999) *Pressure Groups*, London: Hodder & Stoughton.

Smith, A. (1930) *The Wealth of Nations*, London: Methuen.

Whitely, P., Seyd, P. and Richardson, J. (1994) *True Blues*, Oxford: Oxford University Press.

Whitely, P. and Seyd, P. (1998) *New Labour–New Grass Roots Party?* Sheffield: University of Sheffield.

JOURNALS

Relevant articles appear in the following journals:

Talking Politics, the Journal of the Politics Association, Old Hall Lane, Manchester M13 0XT.

Politics Review, Philip Allan publishers, Market Place, Deddington, Oxfordshire OX15 0SE.

Developments in Politics, Causeway Press Ltd., PO Box 13, Ormskirk, Lancashire L39 5HP.

Parliamentary Affairs, Oxford University Press, Great Clarendon Street, Oxford OX2 6DP, in association with the Hansard Society for Parliamentary Government, St. Philips Building North, Sheffield St, London WC2A 2EX.

WEBSITES

Relevant websites include:

http://www.conservative.party.org.uk
http://www.labour.org.uk
http://www.libdems.org.uk

CONFERENCES

One-day conferences are currently organised by, for example:

Enterprise Education Conferences, 4 Princess Road, London NW1 8JJ. Tel: 0207 483 1349.

Student Educational Conferences, Weavers Lodge, The Green, Stalham, NR12 9QA. Tel: 01692 582565/582770.

The Politics Association (see previous address). Tel: 0161 256 3906.

Easter Revision Conferences are also provided by Student Educational Conferences and the Politics Association in London and Manchester.

EXAMINING BOARDS' PUBLICATIONS

Syllabuses, Specimen Papers and Mark Schemes, Teachers' Guides, Question Papers, Mark Schemes and Chief Examiners' Reports.

INDEX

Numbers in **bold** refer to pages on which there is a definition in the glossary.